KEEP GOING

KEEP GOING

From Grief to Growth

Aimee DuFresne

BALBOA.
PRESS
A DIVISION OF HAY HOUSE

Balboa Press books may be ordered through booksellers or by contacting:

Balboa Press
A Division of Hay House
1663 Liberty Drive
Bloomington, IN 47403
www.balboapress.com
1-(877) 407-4847

ISBN: 978-1-4525-7043-3 (sc)
ISBN: 978-1-4525-7045-7 (hc)
ISBN: 978-1-4525-7044-0 (e)

Library of Congress Control Number: 2013904431

Printed in the United States of America

Balboa Press rev. date: 08/26/2013

To my Ben,
When you left my heart shattered into a million tiny pieces.
Over time the pain ground them into sand in my soul.
And one day a gust of change blew them out
And allowed my heart to be shared with the world.
Thank you, Ben, for being you, and for loving me.
I am lucky and privileged to have shared nearly
one-third of your life with you.
Your spirit is always with me, inspiring me to keep going.
Thank you for loving me,
Believing in me,
And teaching me how to live.
And to Lily, to give you a glimpse of your amazing Uncle Ben.

He Is Gone
You can shed tears that he is gone
Or you can smile because he has lived.
—David Harkins

Acknowledgments

I wish to express my sincere gratitude to everyone who helped this book come to fruition. Without the support I received from friends and family after this tragedy, I wouldn't still be here to have finished this project. My deepest gratitude to Alyson and Kevin, Glyn and Sue, Scott, Helen, Joe and George, Ian and Janet, Jay and Tracy, Janet and Roger, Stephen and Liz, Sandra and Sham, Des and Alice, Liz and Emily, Hannah and Pedram, and Jennie and Simon. Special thanks to Dawn Tedder for suggesting I write this amazing love story.

Thanks to my mom for sticking with me through the tears and the anger, and for continuing to encourage me to write and being so willing to read every word.

And to my Mumsy, who knows the perfect thing to say or do in any situation, or not say and not do. It's a difficult balance, but you continue to manage it effortlessly.

My gratitude for all those I have met in my "new life" and who encouraged and assisted me along the way. Emily Lilley, who listened to my countless stories with interest and edited many versions of my writings with honest feedback. To all my Fearless Friday guests whose inspiring stories allowed me to drop my fear around sharing something so personal with the world. To Denise and Meadow Linn; the enthusiasm, wisdom, and pure joy you have for life and helping others is contagious. Thank you. To Peter

Klein, my mentor/coach/guru, who, when I set a deadline of six months, cut it down to one month and believed in me every step of the way. To Balboa Press, for enabling me to share my message with the world. And to the team at Double Image Studio and Vanessa Lowry for capturing my vision on the cover.

Many thanks to Farouk, my "Moon": thank you for finding me in my darkest hour and being my friend, for your patience, and for lighting up a whole new world of adventure while still honoring my past. You continue to amaze with each passing day. I love you.

My deepest gratitude to Lily. Know that even when I am not with you, you are always in my thoughts and I love you more than mere words can describe. Let my life be a lesson that you can find joy even if you endure the greatest sorrow. May this book show what true love looks like and may you find true love in your own life. Let no one's negativity detract you from your dreams or perceived slights ever stand in your way. Always remember, you hold the power to make life magical. Love and light always surround you. Always.

Many thanks to my dad. I still hear your words of wisdom in my head all the time. I was listening! I miss you, and I'm doing my best to make you proud. Thanks for being such a great role model and for sending me so many rainbows.

And thank you to my sunshine, Ben. I could write a whole book thanking you. Oh wait, I think I just did that. ☺ I love you.

Introduction

While some years pass you by or blur into the next, there are those that are engraved on your brain and you remember forever. These years change you, and you are never the same.

For me, that year was 2008. Riding a wave of great happiness, I celebrated my thirtieth birthday in January with a surprise trip to Iceland with my husband. In March, we traveled to France with family and feasted on French cuisine.

But in April, the tide turned, throwing me off balance and into uncharted waters, beginning with the death of my dad. I clung to my husband, Ben, like a life preserver, but in July, he suddenly slipped away to the afterlife.

It was then that I had a choice. I could cry and lie down and die, or I could use what I had learned from him to keep going and fully live.

Ben lit up my life for the eight years we spent together. Even on the dreariest days in London, he was my sunshine. I came to realize that even when you don't see the sun, it still exists. And it exists in each of us.

By sharing this story with you, it is my intent that you become a stronger swimmer in your own life and better equipped to handle treacherous waters. Whatever loss, pain or tragedy you have experienced, you can get through. When things are not going as you had hoped or expected, chances are life has a lesson to teach you. Are you willing to learn from it?

For I believe there is a hidden gift in having your greatest fears become a reality, and there is a hidden gift contained in the story that unfolds in the pages to follow. I hope that you find it and it lights up your world.

Prologue

Now comes the night
Feel it fading away
And the soul underneath
Is it all that remains?
—"Now Comes the Night,"
Rob Thomas

Aimee's words read at Ben's life celebration—July 2008

Ben was the most amazing person I have ever met. He had loads of energy and inspired me. He was enthusiastic and always packed in as much as possible in his life, whether it was traveling, rock climbing, cycling challenges, swimming, photography, cooking, or advancing his career. He was passionate and loved life. I had not started "living" life until I met Ben.

We spent eight fantastic years together. The life we shared in those years was brilliant. We moved from the States to England and traveled extensively in the UK, as well as visiting France, Germany, Portugal, Italy, Spain, and Australia. We tried new things together: snorkeling, hot-air ballooning, rock climbing, and parasailing, to name a few. Life was always an adventure. We went through tough times, but we got through them together and always came out stronger and closer because of them. I told Ben every day that I was the luckiest girl in the world to be his wife and to have his love.

Whenever I was unsure or worrying about what to do in a situation, Ben would say, "Aimee, stop analyzing everything so much and *just do it*! Everything will be okay." Ben could always see the positive in any situation.

It would have been a wasted eight years if I didn't take what I learned from Ben and apply it to my life. Ben, for you I promise to go on living life. I hope to inspire people the way you inspired me with your energy and enthusiasm. I know you'll be with me, helping me along the way. People keep saying it is unfair and you were taken too soon. I would have been honored to have you with me for eight hundred years, but that would have been selfish. I know there must be a better place, and you deserve to be in the best place. You were always in a hurry to get to great places. You won the race, Ben. Enjoy your victory.

Chapter 1

The light from the window is fading
You turn on the night
The sound from the avenue's calling you
Open your eyes
—"My, My, My," Rob Thomas

London, July 17, 2008

T he sound of the doorbell followed by a knock broke
through my sleep. Still hazy, and slightly annoyed by
the intrusion, I opened my eyes and wondered why Ben
would be ringing the doorbell. Surely he had his key. Why would
he wake me up this late?

The doorbell rang again, followed by more knocks that led to
greater confusion. I stumbled out of bed and fumbled to put on
my robe. The doorbell rang yet again, and suddenly something
felt wrong . . . *very wrong*. I rubbed my eyes and looked at the
clock—2:37 a.m. It was 2:37 a.m.? Ben had promised to be home
from his work event by eleven o'clock at the latest. He was never
this late. I hesitated.

The doorbell rang again. I finally went to look out the window
to see what I had hoped not to see: a police car parked in front
of the house. Again the doorbell rang, followed by more knocks,

this time much more insistent. I slowly made my way down the stairs and to the front door.

As I walked down the stairs, a million thoughts went through my head. Maybe Ben had been caught speeding, and the police gave him a ride home after taking away his license? I opened the door and there was no Ben, only two police officers, crushing my theory. Maybe they had put Ben straight in jail. Okay, this seemed unlikely, as Ben was an upstanding citizen and had never been in trouble with the law. He was the most decent human being I had ever met. Maybe it wasn't about Ben at all. Perhaps the police had come to the wrong house by accident.

"Mrs. Morgans?" asked the male officer.

Okay, perhaps not.

I nodded weakly as I looked past the officers, hoping to catch a glimpse of Ben in the back of their cruiser. The car was empty. My body was frozen in the doorway.

"May we come in?" asked the female officer.

I nodded again, my face a mask of confusion as I moved aside to let them in. My body felt like lead, but my mind was racing. All right, so there had been an accident. But we could get through this. Ben and I had been through difficult times, and we always became stronger as a result. We had been through so much recently, with Dad passing away after a long battle with cancer just a few months ago. Ben had been my pillar of strength during this time, and I would be his now.

Had he been badly hurt? Was he paralyzed? In a coma? My mind raced to various solutions to each of these scenarios. I recalled stories of people who had been told they would never walk again but miraculously made full recoveries. Similar stories about coma patients came to mind. Whatever it was, I would do my utmost to ensure Ben was comfortable and help him heal. We would find a way through this. It couldn't be that bad. We had vowed to be together forever, and I was prepared to keep my promise, whatever it took.

"Let's go sit down," said one of the officers, guiding me through the hallway and into the living room. *Why weren't they telling me what had happened?*

"Is Ben okay?" I asked, panic rising in my heart and voice.

"Let's go sit down," the officer repeated.

"*Tell me he's okay!*" I stopped in my tracks, waiting for an answer. Why were they being so cruel? Why didn't they just tell me how bad it was so I could plan solutions and go see Ben?

The officers exchanged a look. "You really should sit down, Mrs. Morgans."

"Tell me he's okay. Just tell me he's fine! I'll sit once you've told me!" I stood adamantly by the couch. I felt that if I didn't sit down, it would somehow be okay.

Realizing I was not going to give in, the male officer sighed and spoke. "I'm afraid Ben has been involved in an accident."

Time stopped. I stood frozen.

"I'm sorry . . . but Ben died."

At that moment, my heart poured out of my chest as I collapsed on the couch. The sound of my screams filled the air.

Chapter 2

Hold on to me
Never leave
Forever be what you mean to me right now
—"My, My, My," Rob Thomas

I n the hours following the accident, I was stuck in the denial stage of grief. I spoke to my brother in Virginia, who assured me that he and his wife were getting the next flight to London to be with me.

"Really?" I responded in disbelief. In my head, I thought they were going to be seriously upset to have spent all that money and time just to arrive and find out Ben was fine. For fear of being thought of as crazy, I kept these thoughts to myself.

There was silence on the line. My brother, still grieving for our dad, broke the silence with truth: "I don't know what to say."

I didn't know either. "It's okay," I responded. "I'll let you go."

He refused and told me he wouldn't get off the line until my friend arrived. The police also would not leave until my friend arrived. I wanted everyone to leave so I could go back to bed and wake up from this nightmare to have Ben's warm body and smiling face beside me.

My friend arrived and, to my surprise, broke down in tears. I was too shocked to respond; I still believed Ben was coming home. My friend did too. We both sat in front of the television, patiently waiting for Ben to walk in and put an end to this whole mess.

"I'm going to kick his ass when he does walk through that door," said my friend. "Then I'm going to give him a big hug." I smiled at the thought of hugging Ben.

The door did open later, but it was not Ben. It was his family. I heard whispers behind closed doors and was aggravated they felt I was too weak to know whatever they were talking about. The police arrived later to explain in greater detail what had happened and the forthcoming proceedings. I lost my breath for a few moments when I learned Ben's helmet had come off when he was thrown from his bike. I gasped for air and tried to keep myself from fainting.

We were also told his death was instantaneous. I found that slightly comforting, having watched my father in so much pain for weeks at the hospice before he passed away, less than three months earlier.

But I still didn't 100 percent believe it was Ben. My mind raced for a plausible scenario. Perhaps Ben's bike had been stolen, and it was the thief who was now lying in the morgue. Maybe the perpetrator knocked Ben out and took his phone and wallet, so poor Ben was just now waking up and walking home. Yes. That could be what happened.

We were asked to go identify the body. I couldn't do it. Just in case it was him. Seeing my dad's body after death was still deeply engraved in my memory. It was just an empty shell; my dad was no longer there. I couldn't bear to see Ben's shell. He was so full of life. I knew it would send me into delirium. Clawing my way back to reality would be difficult, if not impossible. Already my grasp on reality was tenuous at best.

As his family headed to the morgue, my friend and I went out for some fresh air. I anxiously awaited the call telling me the body was not Ben's.

That call never came.

Chapter 3

I tried my best to keep a brave face on in front of friends and family, so they wouldn't know how broken I was inside. That evening, once alone in my bed—our bed—the pain rushed out of me like a tidal wave. I cried and cried. Oceans of tears flowed down my cheeks, and it literally felt as if my heart was being ripped out of my chest. The sobs were earthquakes of my soul, and the tremors rocked my body. I tried to calm the waters, so I wouldn't wake up my mother-in-law sleeping in the guest room.

Memories washed over me with brutal force. There were so many happy memories: the day we met in New York City, our first kiss, traveling to London together, the proposal, the wedding, buying our first home and our bed. We had picked the bed out together after visiting many stores and had spent more money on it than anticipated because "we deserved it." That bed was now my raft in these treacherous waters, the sheets we had so carefully chosen now smothering me in an abyss of anguish.

My feeble attempts to keep my storm of sorrow silent were useless. I heard footsteps, and the door opened. Ben's mum's arms wrapped around me, and we rode the waves together until the sun came up. We had washed up on new land. A land without her son. A land without my husband.

Chapter 4

I didn't hear you leave
I wonder how am I still here
I don't want to move a thing
It might change my memory
—"Here With Me," Dido

"I'm never changing these sheets."

Ben's mum and I lay in bed, under the striped blue duvet cover Ben and I had chosen together months before. Ben and I loved that it matched the shades of blue we had painted our bedroom: one wall a deep blue, the others pale. We got the idea from a painting we had bought together when visiting Wales. The painting was actually three small paintings of brushstrokes in blue, brown, and white, reminiscent of a beach, contained in one white frame. The glass over the images had broken during the move to our home. We had only just got around to fixing it a few weeks before. The glass was smooth and clear now, but our life together was broken. The varying shades of blue that had once provided peace and tranquility were now vicious waves of memories drowning me in sorrow.

The mere thought of changing the sheets filled me with terror. We had slept together in these sheets. There was still part of him here, no matter how small. How could I wash that away? I clung to it as if I were holding on to a piece of driftwood in the middle of a vast ocean.

In the morning, neither Ben's mum nor I wanted to leave the comfort of the bedroom. I brought up tea and toast with jam, and we ate in bed. Ben's mum accidentally dropped a piece of toast on the bed. The raspberry jam was like blood in the ocean. Before my mind could stop me, my mouth let out a scream. *"I told you I'm not washing the sheets! Ever!"*

She quickly picked up the toast and cleared the red stain with her napkin. "It's fine," she assured me. "See? It's all gone. You don't ever have to wash the sheets. Don't worry."

I set down my own plate and cup and collapsed beside her on the bed, exhausted. I didn't want to yell. I didn't want to be in a world without Ben.

Ben's mum finished her toast and tea and put the empty cup and plate on the floor beside her. She looked at me with kind eyes and told me I was the best thing that ever happened to her son.

I was astounded. Ben was surely the best thing that ever happened to me. How could she be so kind to me, especially after I had just yelled at her? I was alive while her son was dead. How could she not want me dead instead? I certainly wanted that. How could she not hate me? She didn't like Ben riding a motorcycle, but I had never stopped him. I always encouraged him to follow his passions. She should have been blaming me for his death, not telling me how lucky he was to have me in his life.

She told me how he "grew up" and became a stronger person after meeting me. He began taking charge of his own life.

It took me back to when I first met Ben. And I shared with her how I met her son, the love of my life.

Chapter 5

Ben, the two of us need look no more
We both found what we were looking for
With a friend to call my own
I'll never be alone
And you my friend will see
You've got a friend in me
—"Ben," Michael Jackson

New York City, May 2000

I'm rushing from class at Hunter College on the Upper East Side down to the Flatiron District, where I work as the night manager at a marketing research center. I walk as a means to get exercise and for the fact that I love walking in the city.

When I arrive at work, the British intern is introducing a new intern. The new boy is about five feet six, stout and muscular, with spiky, light brown hair and a big, yet slightly nervous, grin on his face. He looks about twelve years old.

"Aimee, meet Ben." The twelve-year-old directs his beaming smile at me and stretches out his hand. As we shake, my thoughts leap out of my mouth. "How old are you, Ben?"

"Twenty-three."

I'm astonished. He's older than me! He looks so young and innocent. I fear New York City will change him. It has certainly changed me. Fearing that grin of sunshine will be wiped from his face, I feel it necessary to warn him, "Don't listen to what anybody says here. Just be you."

Ben's smile remains intact, but his eyes show some confusion. He thanks me for the advice, even though he doesn't quite understand it.

As the months pass, I'm glad to see Ben's smile remain intact and his enthusiasm grow. He covers the reception area while the receptionist is at lunch, and I get used to seeing his smiling face greet me each day as the elevator doors open. He is the only intern who does the job and does not complain about it. He is the only staff member in the company who does not complain. He is the assistant to the owner, who treats people harshly in word and in action. But Ben doesn't seem to notice. I'm amazed by him and feel compelled to be around him more.

In the evenings, Ben covers reception for the few hours before closing. Reception being near my office, we often strike up conversations during slow periods. I learn Ben is from Reading, England. I have heard about England from the other interns; it sounds like a magical place. I hope to visit one day.

I share with Ben that I have been in NYC five years and am bored. Ben is stunned that I am in the most exciting city in the world and am bored. I explain to Ben my daily routine. I wake up early to attend classes until late afternoon, when I walk to work and finish by midnight. I am home by 1:00 a.m. and go straight to bed, to wake up early and do it all again. It is the same day in and day out. I crave new experiences.

Ben listens. That is perhaps the most profound thing he does throughout our years together. He listens. Listens without judging, without telling me what to do, without brushing me off or trying to find a solution. He listens without thinking he knows what I am going to say. He opens his ears and his eyes and clears his thoughts. He truly listens.

Ben is gone. Who will listen to me now?

Chapter 6

London, July 2008

I desperately missed talking to Ben. It had always been us against the world. We were true partners. Now I felt a huge chunk of myself was missing. In a weak attempt to retrieve it, I picked up a pen and one of the three orange, red, and black-striped notebooks we had bought together recently to write down all our goals and dreams. I took a deep breath and began to write.

19th July 2008

Dearest Ben,

I miss you so much it hurts everywhere. It feels like my heart is literally being ripped out. When the doorbell rang that night, I thought, "Why are you ringing the doorbell? How could you get home on your bike and not have your house key?" I was so disoriented. I looked at the bed and thought you must already be there. I saw the clock read well after two, and you told me you would be home by 11:00 p.m. When I saw the police car outside, I prayed that you had only broken the law and they were bringing you home on a warning. Or maybe your bike broke down and they kindly gave you a ride home. But I didn't see you there.

I want to be with you so bad. How can you just be gone? We had so many plans. We were going to Turkey and to Thailand and skiing! You were doing the Bananaman and the triathlon, and we were running the Nike Human Race 10K at Wembley.

How can it be over so quickly? We made sure you had the best motorcycle gear, and you promised it was safe. You promised!

Remember a few days earlier I saw the bike racer on TV come off, and he bounced and skidded but was fine. His helmet didn't come off. How did yours?

You were my life, my world; you meant everything to me. I would have happily died for you. You had so much you gave to the world to make it a better place, and I know you weren't finished.

I got your orthotics fixed on Wednesday. I left them out for you on the ottoman so you could see them when you got home. I couldn't stop staring at them throughout the morning, and I couldn't move them. I still hoped you would come home and see them.

I peeled satsumas so I could make you pineapple/satsuma juice in the morning. I also made raw walnut burgers to have for dinner on Thursday (you are probably glad you missed those . . . ;-).

I still think you are coming home (even though I know it's not true). Why don't you take me with you so we can be together again? How can I live my life without you?

I miss kissing you in the morning before I go to work. Especially when you are still in bed, sleepy and dreamy and totally gorgeous.

I had already bought your birthday card and was making plans for a weekend celebration. I wanted to take you somewhere special while also avoiding the bank holiday traffic. I wanted it to be luxury and relaxation because that is what you deserved. I was taking you to brunch on Saturday at Sam's Brasserie, and then we would be off to Canary Wharf for a romantic package at the Four Seasons Hotel! Complete with champagne and chocolate-covered strawberries! The room with a view of the Thames! I was so looking forward to spending time alone with you. Life was so busy. Without you, time has stopped.

I miss you so much, Ben. I ate a cheeseburger, onion rings, and a chocolate milk shake in your honor today at Hamburger Union in Leicester Square. We toasted you and your fantastic life. My family took me to see Spamalot. *It starred the guy from* Meet the Kumars *that you liked so much. Although the show was funny, I cried because I wanted you to be there and felt guilty for trying to have fun without you.*

I love you more than words can say. I want to beg you to come back. I want to be with you again . . . forever. Please help me through this; I don't know how to live in a world without the bright light and love of my Ben.

I love you forever,
Aimee

In the days and weeks following the accident, I stared at a picture of us taken at his family's home. We are both in blue shirts, our blue eyes shining and smiles beaming. We are so happy. Ben looked so alive. How could he possibly be gone? I sat on our bed with the picture cradled in my arms and stared at his beautiful face as I repeated over and over again, "Please take me with you. Take me with you. Take me with you."

I hoped and prayed he was listening, like he always did.

Chapter 7

I found a way to let you in
But I never really had a doubt
Standing in the light of your halo
I got my angel now
—"Halo," Beyoncé

NYC, 2000

I arrive at work one day to Ben's beaming face, and he tells me to "get ready, girly." I'm confused.

"You said you were bored doing the same thing day in and day out, so I have arranged for us to do something new and exciting. Rock climbing at Chelsea Piers."

I'm surprised and touched. *Wow, he really did listen.* He hands me a sheet of paper with all the info.

"Thursday night is ladies' night. You can get in for half price. Get ready. We are going this Thursday." It's a statement, not a question. For the first time in a long time, I'm actually excited.

Before I can read too much into this outing together, Ben says, "Feel free to bring your friends along." It's clear this is just a friendly outing, and I'm eager to go.

My friends decline the invitation, but I maintain my excitement. I go out to purchase a suitable outfit for the event. I take time and great care picking out the perfect activewear top and cargo pants. For reasons I cannot quite comprehend, I feel getting ready for this outing deserves this high level of attention.

When the big day arrives, I put on my perfect outfit and cover it with a T-shirt and jacket. We head off to Chelsea Piers.

We arrive and split the cost of the half-price lady's ticket and the full-price ticket. Ben appreciates the gesture, saving him a few bucks. I appreciate him listening and arranging this outing.

I get a bit nervous about showing off my new outfit and consider leaving on my baggy T-shirt. Ben heads off like a kid in a candy shop and starts bouncing on a trampoline. "Hey, look at me!" he shouts as he bounces up and down like Tigger from *Winnie-the-Pooh*. I feel so comfortable with Ben. I let go of my fears and my baggy T-shirt, revealing my modest activewear top. Ben looks around at me, does a double take, falls over on the bouncy surface, and then quickly recovers. He's only seen me in baggy clothes before. He plays off his reaction as we walk to the climbing wall, and I silently congratulate myself for picking the perfect outfit.

Although we are not on a date, I still feel some anxiety about being harnessed up and climbing a wall with Ben around. I want to show I am athletic yet graceful. I finally get to the top of the wall with my dignity intact. I realize I now have to get down.

The guide helping us and handling the ropes yells up to me to lean back and put all my weight on the harness. He assures me he can hold all my weight, but I'm hesitant. I lean back and put about half my weight in his hands. This turns out to be a bad idea. When I do start to abseil down, the additional weight is a surprise to my guide. My way down is fast. My butt slams the floor along with my dignity. Ben and the guide rush to my side to ensure I am okay. So much for being graceful.

After our rock climbing session, we head to Häagen-Dazs, where Ben shares with me his love of ice cream. We indulge in cookie-dough ice cream and have a nice chat before going out in the cold. As we start to walk, I feel a little tingly, and it's not from the cold. I think I kinda like Ben. *Like* him like him. I wonder if he feels the same.

We come up to the train station and I tell him this is my stop. I prepare for a for a hug or an "I had a great time; see you soon." Ben surprises me by doing neither. He doesn't even stop walking. Turning his head over his shoulder, he says, "Okay, bye," and continues on his way.

I go home, happy for our time together, confused as to how I feel, and wondering how Ben feels.

Chapter 8

Let your bright light shine
Let your words live on
Far beyond this life
Beyond this life
—"My, My, My," Rob Thomas

England, July 2008

We were scheduled to meet a celebrant to plan Ben's funeral. With my brother navigating the car on the unfamiliar left side of the road, we set off for Ben's dad's home. On the motorway, a strange feeling came over me, like I was being smothered by a big blanket of sadness. I looked out the window and realized we were passing the exact spot where Ben was thrown off his motorbike. I took a deep breath and tried to ignore the elephant sitting on my chest.

We arrived, and the family (both Ben and my own) sat around, making idle conversation that ended in stunted silences. I thought back to what Ben and I had discussed when my father died. I asked Ben what he wanted at his funeral. He said he wanted no tears, only bright colors (no black allowed), and he wanted a big party to celebrate his life. "After all," he said, "I love my life. So people should celebrate that." Although his life celebration was happening decades earlier than I ever could have imagined, I was determined to fulfill his wishes.

When the celebrant arrived, I explained Ben's wishes to him. He nodded through my explanation. When I finished, he said, "Well, he is dead and gone. It's sad. It shouldn't be too much of a celebration."

His words took the breath from me, like I'd just been punched where my heart used to be. I excused myself and made it to the bathroom just in time for the tears to burst from my eyes. I had no idea how long I was in there. I tried my best to compose myself quickly, and returned in time to see the man leave.

I asked Ben's dad to find another celebrant. Thankfully, he agreed.

The new celebrant asked if it would be okay, given the circumstances of Ben's death, that the celebrant rode in on a motorcycle.

I smiled. We had found the perfect man to lead the celebration of Ben's life.

Chapter 9

NYC, 2000

After our rock-climbing adventure, the weeks go on, and our friendship grows. Our evening talks at the reception desk become routine.

One evening, the subject of family comes up. "My family is rather different than most," Ben admits. "Some might say it's weird."

My competitive nature is roused as I think of my own family. "I bet mine is weirder than yours."

Ben accepts the challenge and begins his case. "My parents are divorced."

I immediately interject that mine are too.

"My dad is with someone new, and so is my mom."

"Both my parents remarried less than six months after their divorce."

"My dad has a four-year-old son. I have a brother who is almost twenty years younger than me."

"My dad has two kids from a previous marriage. I have a sister and a brother who are about ten years older than me."

"I have a sister and a stepbrother who are ten years younger than me."

"Between my parents, there have been a total of seven marriages. Dad was married four times and Mom is on her third marriage."

Ben's eyes widen in surprise as he takes in a sharp breath of air. Our blue eyes lock on each other for an extended moment.

"You win," Ben concedes.

Leaving the reception area to return to my office, I'm surprised, and pleased, that our broken homes have brought us closer together.

Chapter 10

No I will not leave you crying
And I will not let you down
—"Now Comes the Night,"
Rob Thomas

July 2008

Dear Ben,

Remember the day we all visited the funeral home so Dad could make his own arrangements?

I had been trying to be strong throughout the days and cry only through the nights. On that day, I could no longer hold back. The tears started when we sat down and they did not stop. Tissue after tissue after tissue. The funeral director went over my dad's life and legacy. She was confirming the names and number of his children when she looked at me and asked, "Are you the baby of the family?" I choke out a sobbing yes and more tears flowed. I was clearly acting like a baby but I couldn't stop. She sent me a sympathetic smile. You squeezed my hand tighter to let me know you were there. I was so grateful for you. It never crossed my mind that you would not be there.

I thought that was the hardest day of my life. Turns out, it wasn't. Now I sit in a similar room discussing a funeral. Without Dad. Without you. They are asking me what casket I would like for you. All I can think of is your favorite color: red.

Days later, I am back in the same place, standing just outside the room where the red box is stored. I gather up all my strength and cross the threshold.

It looks small. We had such big dreams, all-encompassing love, and so many memories. How could all this be stored in such a little box?

"Are you okay in there?" I asked, lightly running my fingers over the red polished box. It reminded me of a Ferrari Formula 1 racing car. Your favorite. I bent down, half expecting an answer. My mind was still on your safety. Did you have enough room? My fingers almost tried to open the box in an attempt to release you, but I knew it was sealed shut and my efforts would be futile.

I sat down and rested my head on the box, just like I used to rest my head on your chest. I wanted you out of the box—or to be in the box with you. I wondered how long they would allow me to stay.

I had no idea if it was minutes or hours later when I heard a small knock, breaking me out of my reverie and back to reality. My brother popped his head around the door. "You okay?" he asked, knowing the question was silly but not knowing what else to say.

I raised my head from the red box, and he came in and sat next to me. I knew I soon needed to leave the red box. The box containing the life I knew, the many memories we shared, and the countless plans we had for our future. When I left that room, I would be leaving so much more than just your body.

My brother and I sat silently for a while. Then, in an attempt to be helpful, he asked me what stage of grief I was in. "Denial? Anger? Acceptance?" He uttered the last word with hopefulness in his voice.

"Guilt."

He looked surprised by my response. His eyes conveyed that he wasn't sure he wanted to know the answer, but still he asked, "Why do you feel guilty?"

"Because for the last six months of Ben's life, all I did was cry about Dad. I was upset the cancer was back. I cried because it was growing. I cried because his health was getting worse by the day. And I cried when he passed. I just cried and cried."

I remembered Ben saying to me on more than one occasion, "Where has my wife gone? You cry so much you are like a different person. I want my Aimee back."

Although I tried to hide it from him, I continued to cry. And he knew me so well; I could never hide things from him.

Later that evening, I asked for absolution.

Please forgive me, Ben. If I had known it was going to be the last six months of your life, I would have spared you and saved all my tears to shed now.

I'll do my best to be "your Aimee."

I love you.
Your wife xxx

Chapter 11

Never thought I'd be alright
'Til you came and changed my life
What was cloudy now is clear
You're the light that I need here.
—"Ain't No Other Man,"
Christina Aguilera

NYC, 2000

"We are going out tonight. You should come with us."

It's a Friday and I have just arrived at the office.

"Who is 'us'?" I ask Ben.

"A group, most of us interns, and a friend who is visiting me from home."

I'm intrigued by the invitation, but I already have plans with the girls in the office. I don't want to cancel; I've been looking forward to catching up with them.

"Bring them with you; the more the merrier." Ben's eyes linger on mine for a long time. This has been happening more often lately. I'm getting the impression he's flirting with me, but I'm not very good at flirting or recognizing when someone else is flirting. Maybe I just want him to be flirting with me.

I ask the girls for their opinions later that evening.

"He's *definitely* flirting with you," says Chantal. "He flirts with you all the time; how do you not see it? He stands closer to you when he talks to you. And the way he talks with you—it's definitely flirting. He wants you."

"*No way!*" says Jenna, to my displeasure. "I don't see that at all. He's happy all the time and he likes *everyone*. I think he might be gay. He did the AIDS fundraising bike ride. Why would you do that if you weren't gay?"

About 90 percent of the men working in our office are, in fact, gay. And Ben did do the AIDS bike ride. If he is gay, that's fine. Still, I like Chantal's answer much better.

"I don't care if he is straight or gay," says Lisa. "He's Ben, and I love him!"

We all cheer to that and clink glasses as we polish off our second . . . or third . . . or fourth drink. Which makes it seem like a perfectly good idea to hop in a cab and join Ben's party at the bar downtown after all. We're on a mission to find out the truth.

Laughing and loud all the way downtown, the four of us stumble out of the cab at the Cowgirl Hall of Fame, where Ben and his friends are meeting. Surprisingly, we see Ben and a friend eating outside at a restaurant down the street. At first I think I have drunk too much and am hallucinating Ben everywhere. But he waves and says he will see us in a minute.

We carry on walking and enter the crowded bar (which I later learn is a lesbian bar—had I known, it would only have confused me further as to Ben's sexual preferences). We find one small, unoccupied table, and the four of us gather around it, waiting for Ben to arrive. Well, at least I am certainly waiting for him to arrive.

About fifteen minutes later he finally does. He comes up to us and thanks us all for coming. All of us. No lingering eyes on me. No beaming smile directed specifically my way. He then tells us he'll see us later and walks away.

The alcohol in my system overrides my common sense and the thought in my head comes screaming out of my mouth. "ASSHOLE!"

"Pardon?" Ben responds in his cute British accent, which only aggravates me more.

"You are an asshole! We came all this way to see you, and now you are walking away!"

My companions sit with jaws dropped, expressions of shock and awe on their faces. I'm normally very timid and quiet.

"Well, I don't think I've ever been called an asshole before." Ben takes a moment to ponder this accusation.

"Well, it's about time you were, then!" I retort. At the back of my mind it's becoming clear I like this guy, and I'm scared of getting hurt.

"I'm sorry you feel that way," Ben responds. He has every right to get angry, but he keeps his calm. "I'd be happy for you guys to come to the back where all my friends and I will be."

"Whatever," I say, turning my nose up and my face away. He looks confused for a moment, repeats that we are all welcome to join them, and heads off to his friends.

As soon as he is out of earshot, my friends turn to gaze incredulously at me. "What the hell was that?" they say in unison.

I have to admit it. "I like Ben, and I want him to like me too."

Clearly this is a time for more alcohol. We buy a pitcher of frozen margaritas from the bar and head to the back to be with Ben and his friends.

The room is large and divided into two areas with couches. One area is full of Ben's friends and the other is free and clear. We take advantage of being close to but not exactly part of his party. Ben does a good job of mingling between both groups, proving what I said to him in anger to be completely untrue.

At around eleven o'clock, Lisa and Jenna announce they are going home, leaving Chantal and me behind with extra room and an empty pitcher of frozen margaritas. I am convinced Ben will stop mingling now that there is only Chantal and me. He will have fun with just his friends. When I confess my fear to Chantal, we make a bet. She believes he likes me and will be back to talk to us. I don't mind paying the price if he does. If she is wrong, at least I will be a few bucks richer. We shake hands to confirm the ten-dollar bet.

Within minutes, my ten dollars is gone and Ben is beside me. Another pitcher of frozen margaritas makes its way to the table. We are laughing and, dare I say, flirting? His big blue eyes look deep into mine as he sits close to me and beams his beautiful smile my way. It is pure sunshine in the dark bar nearing midnight. I feel like the luckiest girl in the world.

When Ben goes back to his friends, Chantal holds out her hand for the ten-dollar bill and confirms he was indeed flirting. Big time. Then, to my disappointment, she announces she has to leave. As she is not familiar with the area, I have promised to take her to the train station. It is time to go.

I go up to Ben to say good-bye, expecting a protest that I should of course stay longer or profuse thanks for an outstanding evening. Instead, he repeats our parting from the night we went rock climbing. With barely a glance over his shoulder, he says, "Bye," and walks away.

With the extra alcohol coursing through my blood making me bold, I repeated my accusation of earlier.

"You *are* an asshole!"

"What?" He turns around, shocked. "Why?"

"Because you flirted with me all night. You clearly like me. Yet you do nothing when I leave?"

Chantal listens from the doorway. Ben just stares at me, speechless.

"Well?"

"Well . . . what?" Ben's blue eyes become perplexed.

"Well, aren't you going to kiss me?" I practically yell in front of all of his friends. Chantal shakes her head in the background, trying to hold back laughter.

Ben's eyes widen in surprise. He nods and steps forward. Closing his eyes, he leans forward to meet my request.

Five minutes later, we are still kissing when Chantal shouts from the doorway, "You guys should have started this earlier. We have to go, Aimee! *Now*! I need to get my train before midnight!"

I am Cinderella and have just found my prince.

Chapter 12

And now, the end is here
And so I face the final curtain
My friend, I'll say it clear
I'll state my case, of which I'm certain
I've lived a life that's full
I traveled each and ev'ry highway
And more, much more than this, I did it my way
—"My Way," Frank Sinatra

London, July 2008

Dear Ben,

I can't believe our fairy tale is over. What happened to "happily ever after"?

I hope you were watching as we celebrated your life. I did everything in my power to make you proud. Your family is amazing and continues to be supportive. They approved of the songs I feel you led me to choose. After the pallbearers (including your sister!) carried you in for your 'final performance', my brother said he couldn't help but smile when he heard Christina Aguilera's voice blare out "Ain't No Other Man."

Your mum shared a beautiful poem, and everyone's words were so kind. You truly made a difference with your life. When we played "My Way" sung by Frank Sinatra (one your favorite singers), everyone, wearing their bright colors, stood up and clapped. I haven't been to many funerals, but I'm guessing that doesn't happen often. You were magical.

People kept asking if the Rob Thomas songs we selected ("My, My, My" and "Now Comes the Night") were written specifically for you. It certainly feels as if they were.

Your siblings got an arrangement of flowers shaped as Tigger, your favorite Disney character and much like your own character of bouncing, boundless energy and having a good time. My family got an arrangement in the form of your favorite brand, Nike, a symbol that reminds us to follow your example and "Just Do It."

My flowers matched your most recent pair of crazy-colored shoes that you had specially made. I remember clearly the day we went to the Nike store in Oxford Circus and you chose the designs you wanted. When they asked you what words you would like to put on the shoes, you looked at me for the answer. I told you they were your shoes and the words should be of your choice. You thought for a moment; then it came to you. "Keep going."

Now I'm looking to you for the answer. How do I keep going without you?

Chapter 13

Somethin' 'bout you caught my eye
Somethin' moved me deep inside
Don't know what ya did boy but ya had it,
And I've been hooked ever since.
—"Ain't No Other Man,"
Christina Aguilera

NYC, October 2000

I'm sitting in front of my computer wondering what to do next. Now sober and more sensible, I wonder if I have forced Ben to kiss me and embarrassed him in front of all his friends. Is he regretting kissing me today? Is he regretting ever inviting me? Is he regretting meeting me?

An e-mail pops up on my screen from Ben, and he asks how I'm doing. After some quick e-mail exchanges, we arrange to meet for a drink later in the week. I'm not scheduled to work until the day after we get together, so thankfully there will be no awkward exchanges at the office beforehand. I'm excited to see Ben but dreading it might be his way of letting me down easy.

We meet outside a bar called Sutton Place. We say hello but avoid looking at each other too long. Our body language is hesitant. We shift uneasily. Without shaking hands, hugging, or touching in any way, we enter the bar, Ben holding the door for me like the gentleman he is.

We sit down, order drinks, and make idle chitchat about the decor of the bar. The conversation turns to what has happened in bars in the past. Ben begins a story of a "friend" who kissed a guy in a bar when she was drunk. I think, "This guy is slick." He is being kind, letting this go and giving me an easy out to explain my bad behavior.

I asked what happened to his "friend" after the drunken evening.

"Oh, she regretted it. She was mortified," Ben answered.

Mortified. That sounded spot-on about how I felt in that moment.

"Want a shot?"

I didn't see that coming. "Um. Sure." He's so nice. He's trying to numb the pain of my embarrassment. A shot suddenly sounds like a great idea.

A few minutes later, Ben returns, a shot in each hand. "These are Screaming Nazis," he informs me.

We clink glasses. Cheers to the numbing of my pain and embarrassment.

We each down our shots, and before I can put my glass on the table, Ben leans over, grabs my face with both his hands, and kisses me so passionately I can feel it all the way down to my toes.

And the kissing continues . . .

Chapter 14

When the hour is upon us
And our beauty surely gone
No you will not be forgotten
No you will not be alone
—"Now Comes the Night,"
Rob Thomas

England, July 2008

I sat in silence, but my brain was full of deafening noise. How could I not remember? I berated myself. How was this possible? So many memories of Ben were flooding through me, but I couldn't recall our last kiss. I knew we had kissed that morning before I left for work. We always did. Why couldn't I remember it? Why couldn't I remember our conversation that morning? It seemed erased from my memory. My fear was that my other memories of Ben would be erased too. "Concentrate. *Concentrate, Aimee!* You can do this. Just remember. It's there."

What felt like an eternity, but in reality was only days later, the memory resurfaced like a message in a bottle washed ashore.

I'm upstairs, gathering the items I need to take to work.
I make my way downstairs, where Ben is working out in the

living room. "Hey, girl," he calls to me when he hears me on the steps. He puts down the weights and meets me at the foot of the stairs.

"Guess what?" I announce as I hold up his orthotics proudly. I work at a chiropractic clinic where a podiatrist visits to see patients twice a month. Ben is a patient and has needed the inserts that were specially made for him to be adjusted slightly. He has been asking me to take the inserts for his shoes in to be repaired.

"You remembered!" Ben exclaims, planting a kiss on my lips. We smile at each other and kiss again before I put all my belongings in my bag and head toward the door. Ben goes to his weights. "Remember, I'm out tonight," he says, lifting alternate weights in a bicep curl. "Quiz night with work. I'll be home by eleven or eleven thirty."

"Okay. Thanks for the reminder. Go kick some ass."

"Yes; I intend to win," Ben says with a smile. "Have fun today! Love you!"

"Love you too!"

I shut the door behind me and think, "I love my life."

Chapter 15

Never knew I could feel like this
Like I've never seen the sky before
Want to vanish inside your kiss
Every day I love you more and more
—"Come What May," Moulin Rouge

NYC, 2000

I love my life. Wow. I have never been this happy . . . ever. Ben brings new adventures and energy to my life. Being with him is like basking in the sunshine on the most beautiful beach.

With Ben, life is suddenly exciting. We walk the streets of Manhattan hand in hand. It is like the world disappears and there is just me and Ben. We enjoy brunch in the city on a Sunday and drinks in the evening. We go to movies. We venture out of the city, having snowball fights at Yale and white-water rafting in West Virginia. I introduce Ben to sushi and he introduces me to his family when they come to visit.

Our usual meeting spot is the World Trade Center. It is convenient, as both our trains are located there. Once we go up to have drinks at the top, but more often we stroll around the stores and restaurants below.

One day, as we stand by one of the pillars at the top of the stairs leading down to the PATH train, we share a kiss. It is more than a kiss. It is magic. Ben later tells me it is in this moment that he realizes he is in love with me.

I clearly remember my thoughts at that moment. As I look around the building, I think how strong the building is and how it will be there forever. Our love seems so fragile. Ben will be going back to England in a few months. We have just been having fun. We haven't expected to fall in love.

But it is love. Ben is the first person I want to see in the morning and the last person I want to see before falling asleep.

Chapter 16

I'll find repose in new ways
Though I haven't slept in two days
'Cause cold nostalgia
Chills me to the bone
—"Vanilla Twilight," Owl City

London, 2008

Dear Ben,

 I lie on the futon in our office/guest room. No longer can I sleep in our bed. No longer can I sleep. The memories are too painful. Every time a motorcycle passes outside, I think for a split second it is you coming home, before the harsh reality hits me like a slap across the face.

 On the rare occasion I do manage to fall asleep, I wake up expecting you to be lying beside me. The crushing truth isn't getting easier over time.

To my surprise, the panic attacks that had accompanied all the stressful situations in my life had yet to come. These attacks had been particularly strong after Dad passed, hitting me unexpectedly. I would feel like an elephant was sitting on my chest, and tears would fall uncontrollably from my eyes as I struggled to catch my breath.

Lying on the futon that morning, I started to feel the familiar pressure on my chest. Bracing myself for the worst, I began the breathing techniques recommended by a friend. To my surprise, the pressure didn't get worse as usual. I realized the feeling was familiar but was not a panic attack. Confused, I continued the breathing exercises and closed my eyes. The feeling was not one of panic at all, but peace. It felt like being held. With my eyes closed, I could feel Ben's presence on top of me, holding me tight, hugging me like he did so many mornings when we woke up.

It crossed my mind that perhaps this was the start of a mental breakdown. But being with Ben (or imagining so vividly that I was) was so delicious that it was worth losing my sanity. I kept my eyes closed and stayed very still, fearing the moment would end the instant I moved.

But the urge to wrap my arms around him was too much. Taking the chance that my arms would only move through thin air, I opened them, hoping to hug Ben back. To my utter surprise, I could feel him!

Wanting to sneak a peek at his beautiful face, I dared to open my eyes. There was only air, but I was still holding on to Ben. I closed my eyes again and ran my fingers up and down the length of his back. I wondered how long this feeling would last. How would I cope when it was over?

Brushing the thought aside, I enjoyed the moment. It was glorious to be together. I felt whole again. No matter if a shattered heart or an insane asylum awaited me, nothing could take away the enjoyment of that moment.

Time vanished. There was only the moment.

At some point, my arms returned to rest by my side. The feeling of Ben's presence slowly dissolved. It was like an energy floating away, blowing me a kiss as it went. Bracing myself for the crushing pain of loss, I was surrounded by only peace, a great sense of peace I had never experienced before. I knew that Ben was happy. I couldn't have asked for more than his happiness. I felt intense gratitude.

As the energy of Ben slipped away, it left behind the whisper: *Everything is going to be fine.*

Chapter 17

Suddenly the world seems such a perfect place
Suddenly it moves with such a perfect grace
Suddenly my life doesn't seem such a waste
It all revolves around you
—"Come What May," Moulin Rouge

NYC to London, May 2001

"It's going to be fine," Ben says to me as we fasten our seat belts on our Virgin Atlantic flight to London.

A worrier by nature, I'm surprised that my feelings don't include worry. That has led to the perplexed look on my face. I am worried about not being worried.

We have been dating for just over six months, and I am on my way to England to live with Ben. It seems crazy. It seems right. Ben has finished his internship and gone on a month-long tour of the West Coast to see more of America. I graduated in January and have been accepted to do the reciprocal internship program for Americans in London. I have worked three jobs to save up for a few months in England before I start the internship in September. I should be scared, but I am far too excited to let in any fear.

"What movies should we watch?" Ben asks as he takes off his shoes, puts on the complimentary slipper socks, and contorts himself into a comfortable position in the economy seat. We watch movies and hold hands for the seven-hour journey to our new home.

Chapter 18

You've gone, I'm here, alone
I guess it's time to grow
—"Time to Grow," Lemar

London, 2008

Months after Ben's death and I was haunted in our own home, surrounded by the life we no longer had. When I opened our closet, my eyes went to Ben's shoes, his shirts and suits. I yearned for him to be back. People kept telling me time heals all wounds, but every opening of the closet door felt like a fresh cut that stabbed me deeper every time. I'd heard it got harder before it got easier. Just when I felt I'd hit rock bottom, the bottom opened up and sucked me down farther. Would I ever stop falling?

November 1, 2008

Ten pairs of sneakers
Thirty ties
Three suits . . .
I collapsed at the head of the stairs this morning, too emotionally spent to walk down the steps. Those steps we playfully chased each other up so many times. The same steps

you used to run down to greet me when I came home from work. It was there that the realization hit me: you are not coming back.

You are never coming back.

And what is worse is you are not coming to get me. I thought if I was strong through this, if I gave you the best life celebration, if I proved to you how strong I am, you would somehow take me with you. I would have earned my place to be with you. You sent me the message that you are happy and I'll be okay. But how am I going to be okay without you?

Remember how I used to call you an angel escaped from heaven? And how if the angels found out, they would try to get you back, but they would have to go through me first? It's not fair. They came and got you while I was sleeping. I was defenseless.

Will I ever be good enough to be with you again? The hole you left where my heart used to be gets bigger every day. Soon there will be nothing left. Just darkness.

I started clearing out your clothes today. I know it's static/ blocked energy to keep them there. As long as they are there, I will still have some hope that you are coming home.

I had a dream last week that you did come back. I was excited to see you, but I couldn't get near you because I didn't want to tell you that you had nothing to wear! I was scared you would hate me for giving away all your stuff. You looked handsome and happy in my dream. That gorgeous smile beaming from your face.

I'm sure you would be equally attracted to me if you saw me right now. Let me paint you the picture: twenty-four hours of nonstop crying, no make-up, hair a mess, and no shower in forty-eight hours. God, I'm sexy.

Strangely, I know if you were here, you would find me sexy, even in my sweatpants that are too large and your oversize sweatshirt. You always saw the beauty in things, no matter how deep down it was hidden.

To prepare to go through your stuff, I put on a meditation CD about "letting go" with Lucinda Drayton. It would have been more helpful if I had been able to stop sobbing so I could hear what she was saying. Once the meditation ended, I composed myself before starting the task. But I immediately lost it again upon opening the door to your side of the closet, falling to the floor in a heap of tears.

I miss you so much. Seeing all your belongings made me miss you even more, which I didn't even think was possible. As I sorted through everything, the weather was dark with high winds and rain. You must have been crying from heaven.

This has been the most difficult thing I have ever had to do. I folded your ties, shirts, suits, and belts, each piece grinding what was left of my heart down into tinier pieces.

Packing up your colorful sneakers was the hardest. I thought about keeping them for a while. I took pictures of all of them lined up and decided to keep one pair, the ones you had made with the words "Keep Going" on them. Advice from my angel. I will do my best.

The sun is shining now. You must be smiling from heaven.

I love you,
Aimee xoxxoxoxo

Chapter 19

I used to say "I" and "me"
Now it's "us," now it's "we."
—"Ben," Michael Jackson

Venice, Italy, July 2001

The sun beats down on our faces as we lean back in the seat on our first gondola ride. Venice is incredible. And incredibly romantic. We are staying the week in Jesolo, a mere boat ride away. It's magical.

During our stay, we hit the beach near our hotel and visit Verona, the land of Romeo and Juliet. Ben urges me to go to up and stand on the famous balcony where it is believed Juliet once stood, but I'm too shy to make my way through the crowd. He settles for snapping a pic of me below it. We hop on boats to see the colorful houses and lacework in Burano, wander around the cathedral in Torcello, and buy our first piece of art together in Murano. After much deliberation and seeing all the beautiful glasswork the island has to offer, we select a delicate blue glass statue of two lovers embracing. We carefully pack it in our suitcase and pray it doesn't break.

Chapter 20

Baby, I can feel your halo
Pray it won't fade away
—"Halo," Beyoncé

London, 2008

Ben,

I look at our glass statue we bought in Italy. It stands proudly on a shelf in our bedroom. Remember how, when we got it home, we were surprised that it was pink instead of blue? The light shining on it in the shop made it take on a blue tinge. Amazingly it has stayed in one piece all these years. A shame I could not say the same of our life together.

In an effort to "Keep Going," I decided I would still run the 10K we signed up for what seems like eons ago.

I went to the gym to train without you, but I could see you in front of me while I ran on the treadmill. "C'mon! You can do it, baby! C'mon; just a little bit farther." The vision of you encouraged me, all the time with that gorgeous, beaming smile. I kept running. I felt a little bit like Forrest Gump.

One day I was feeling particularly alone and lost. I stepped on the treadmill, turned the music on my iPod full blast, and ran.

I ran from my painful present without you. I ran faster from the fear about my future without you, and hoped against hope that I could somehow catch up to you if only I ran fast enough.

As I continued full speed ahead, the music in my ears suddenly stopped. I took out my earphones just as a familiar song started on the gym's sound system. One of "our" songs. I slowed down the treadmill as I listened more closely to the words of the song:

> Just keep trying and trying
> It's just a matter of timing
> Though the grinding is tiring
> Don't let 'em stop you from smiling

As I have never heard Kelis's "Lil Star" played at the gym before or since, I'm rather sure it was you sending me a message. Especially as, when I looked down at my iPod, I saw it was fully charged. That didn't explain why it stopped abruptly. Or how, when the song was finished, the iPod immediately came back on.

Okay, I hear you! I'll do my best to heed your advice.

The date of the race loomed. I was nervous but determined to finish, even if I didn't finish in the time we had set. Your words echoed in my ears: "We can do it in under an hour. No problem. It will be easy." Easy for you to say. Where were you then?

In the days leading up to the race, I picked up our race packs. I took your shirt out of the bag, held it up, and cried. Red. Your favorite color. Each race pack came with a chip to attach to your shoelaces. It recorded the time when you passed the start line and again when you passed the finish line. The officials then texted your official race time.

I untied my laces and restrung them, securing my race chip on my right sneaker. I placed your race chip on my left. You weren't getting out of racing with me after all.

Rain poured from the sky the morning of the race. I kept my fingers crossed it would stop and the sun would come out. It did stop, but the sky was still dark when Leslie knocked on the door. "Ready to go?" She smiled. "We'll make him proud!" I can't honestly say that I was ready, but I did intend to make you proud.

As we began the walk to the train station, the heavens opened and there was a torrential downpour. Perhaps it was you crying from heaven. Whether they were tears of sadness for not being there or tears of laughter watching me do this on my own, I'm not sure. Either way, we were soaked to the bone upon arriving at the train station. We tried to wring out our running clothes as much as possible before boarding the Tube.

During the ride we made small talk. We laughed. Leslie pondered over the course while I refused to look at it, fearing that if I did, I would scare myself out of ever being able to complete it. Better not to know . . .

We arrived at our destination and joined the sea of red-shirted runners. Though the rain had stopped, the sky remained gray. We made our way to Wembley Stadium to check in. Attaching our race numbers to our shirts, we made our way into the stadium and took seats to listen to a band that was on the main stage. The acoustics from where we sat made the music sound like screaming to me. It was anything but calming. I wanted it to stop. I wanted everything to stop. Then I wanted to press the rewind button on time and pick you up from the past so you would be here with me now.

"Leslie," I said as we made our way to the starting line like cattle to the slaughter, "can you do me a favor? Run with me?" You always ran with me during races. We were a team.

"Sure thing," Leslie responded, her gaze on the starting line. We were approaching quickly. Here we go . . .

My feet passed over the bar marking our starting time. Leslie and I started side by side. There were so many red-shirted runners, we soon got separated. Leslie raced her way through the crowd and found her pace. She was a strong runner. It had been unfair to ask her to slow down for me. Now I was exactly where I was afraid of being. Alone.

It started to rain again. I was grateful as it hid the tears coming down my face.

As I continued running, something in me changed. Fear was replaced by calmness. I kept running, and I actually started feeling good. I no longer wheezed as I found own pace. Astoundingly, I started to feel happy. This was fun! Never had running been fun before!

The 7K marker came and went. Then the 8K, then the 9K. The cool rain was welcome on the heat of my skin. My sneakers splashed through puddles. It was fun playing in the rain. My eyes could soon see the finish line as my feet raced to catch up to it. I was nearly there!

Then, just as in front of the treadmill, there you were again, cheering me on. "C'mon, baby! You are nearly there! Just a little farther now!" It felt like the slow-motion button had been pressed as my feet glided over the finish line. I had run 10K!

Leslie was up ahead, clutching the T-shirt given out to everyone who finished. Her eyes scanned the crowd. A race volunteer handed me one of the T-shirts as I made my way to Leslie. "We did it!" I cried as we embraced.

"I'm so sorry I lost you back there," she apologized. "I thought you were right behind me!"

"It's okay," I replied. I had needed to do this on my own. It felt good. It felt right.

My phone started to vibrate in my pocket. A text message. I retrieved it and read: "Congrats on finishing the 10K. Your official race time is 59 minutes and 20 seconds." I had done it! Achieved something I thought impossible.

Then the phone buzzed again, this time with your chip number. "Congrats on finishing the 10K. Your official race time is 59 minutes and 21 seconds." Even more impossible! I beat your time (no wonder you were crying up there). Looks like there is a whole wide world of possibility. Thank you for allowing me to see it.

Who knows? Maybe I will run a marathon next! ;-) I'm learning to live life to the fullest, as one never knows what lies ahead.

Forever yours,
Aimee

Chapter 21

These twists and turns of fate
Time falls away
But these small hours
These little wonders still remain
—"Small Wonders," Rob Thomas

September 11, 2001

"A plane hit the Twin Towers!"

It's my second day at work in Central London. My office is located in the posh area of Mayfair, near Buckingham Palace. There is a second office a few blocks from first. I've come over to the second office today to receive training. That's where I hear the receptionist's scream.

Initially, I'm confused. Surely, they can't be talking about *the* Twin Towers, the strong building where Ben and I fell in love. That can't be right. That can't be possible. Maybe there are Twin Towers in England that I have just never heard about until now.

"Oh my God! Another one has hit!"

The woman training me looks at me with a worried glance. "You're not from New York . . . are you?" It seems the impossible has happened.

When I arrive back at my office, where everyone knows I did come over from New York, deep breaths and uneasy looks greet me. My manager seems flustered. "I know," I answer her before she asks the dreaded question.

I hear the television in the conference room. "Oh, don't go, Aimee. Really, it will only upset you." My manager tries to protect me from seeing the destruction, but I can't stop myself. I head into the conference room just in time to hear a colleague comment, "Bloody time America got hit." He sees me standing silently in the doorway, my eyes fixed on the television. "Well, England always gets hit," he goes on. "We are used to this stuff here, that's all I'm saying. I'm sure they evacuated everyone before anyone got hurt."

Moments later we watch as both towers crumble to the ground. I think of my friends. I fear for my family as the news begins to report more plane crashes.

In a daze, I ride the train home. Ben meets me at the station. I get in the car, and we hold on to each other as we both start to sob.

The Twin Towers no longer exist.

Our love is stronger than ever.

Chapter 22

And when you find
You're spending your time
Wanting for words
But never speak
You tell yourself
That the things you need come slow
But inside you just don't know
—"My, My, My," Rob Thomas

London, 2008

Dear Ben,

I went back to work at the clinic about a month after you left. My boss was nice and offered to give me as much time as I needed, but what I needed was some kind of normalcy, even though nothing will ever be "normal" again.

It hasn't been easy. Some patients have burst into tears at the sight of me. Others want to know every detail. Some pretend they don't know or that it didn't happen. I prefer the latter reaction, as I too would like to pretend that this didn't happen. That when I leave work, you will still be waiting for me at home. You'll come running down the stairs to greet me or be in the kitchen working on your newest culinary creation for dinner. We will eat dinner in the living room and chat about our days with the television on in the background. For dessert, I will try something from my raw vegan recipes, and you will counter with a traditional sweet. Remember when we had our brownie competition? You certainly won that one.

For your life celebration, I asked my brother to make your famous brownies along with your carrot cake. I could never resist those, no matter how "good" I was trying to be with my diet. That day was no different. I bypassed all the other food served and loaded my plate with brownies. As I bit into one, I felt closer to you.

I used to tell you they were filled with toxic ingredients. Maybe if I eat enough of them, I can be with you again. What a way to go: Death by chocolate.

Remember how we could never finish a bottle of champagne between us? Well, now I can finish one all by myself! In fact, I just did. All those bottles we had saved for "special occasions." Well, you missed out. It was good champagne. Don't worry, I'm saving a bottle to drink on your birthday.

Remember all the fun we used to have on birthdays?

Your drunk wife,
Aimee

Chapter 23

Ain't no other man
Can stand, up next to you
Ain't no other man, on the planet
Does what you do
You're the kinda guy, a girl finds
In a blue moon
—"Ain't No Other Man,"
Christina Aguilera

January 2002

My first birthday in England. Determined not to rely solely on Ben and to make friends independently, I schedule a girls' evening out with some fellow American interns the Friday before the big day. Ben calls me at work a few days before.

"I was thinking I would meet you in London on Friday," he says cheerily.

"I would, honey, but I already made plans with the girls. Another night would be great."

There is a brief silence on the line. "Oh. Well, you should consider rescheduling with the girls."

"No, no, this is the first girls' event I have scheduled. I haven't taken the chance to get to know them properly, so this is a great opportunity. If I blow it now, I might never make friends!"

Ben, always understanding, surprisingly doesn't give up. "Well, I don't think you want to miss this."

Getting slightly exasperated, I ask, "What is so important about it being this Friday?"

"Well, I was going to surprise you, but I guess I'll tell you now. I won tickets to dinner and a West End show. The dinner is at this really fancy restaurant I know you will love. I wouldn't want to share it with anyone but you."

Dating just over a year and the man knew me well. My weakness is fine food and theater. Being an intern means eating on a budget, and I don't want to miss out on an opportunity to enjoy something a bit more upscale than Sainsbury's sale items.

"It's only available on Friday," he said, knowing full well I will cave at this point.

"Well . . . let me see what I can do. God, I hate being the girl who cancels plans with the girls to go out with a boy."

"Sorry. I know. If I could make it any other night, I would. I was looking at the menu, and they have this decadent chocolate dessert that has . . ."

"Okay, okay, okay . . . I'll call and cancel." He has me at "chocolate." "Where should we meet? At my office? At the restaurant?"

"Let's meet at Waterloo Station."

"Really? Why? That doesn't make sense." I don't know London that well yet, but I know that Waterloo Station is an awkward place to meet, given the location of the restaurant and the West End show.

Always knowing what to say, Ben replies, "Well, yes, it is farther away, but we will have a little extra time. We can have a romantic walk along the Thames."

Awww . . . my heart melts. "Okay, we'll meet at Waterloo."

Friday comes around and I bid adieu to my work colleagues. We wish each other a good weekend and I am off.

Standing in Waterloo Station, my eyes search the crowd for the familiar face. Through the masses of people, I think I spot him. No, that is not him; that guy is holding luggage. Wait a minute. That piece of luggage looks very familiar.

He spots me too and we walk toward each other. A confused look spreads across my face as I wonder what on earth he is carrying in the bag.

"Fancy going to Paris?" Ben asks, a big grin lighting up his face.

"Now?" I ask in disbelief. Is this really happening? The place I have been dreaming of visiting since I was a little girl?

"Yes."

"Is my stuff in the bag too?"

"Yes."

"We are going now?" I am in a state of shock. This is even better than a decadent chocolate dessert at an upscale restaurant. "For how long?"

"Four days."

"Really?"

"Yes."

I can't believe this is happening. My mind is racing! My bag is packed and I am going to Paris!

Wait! Suddenly I think of work and how I need this job to stay in the country. "Oh no! I have to work on Monday!"

"No, you don't. I called your work and got you the day off."

Whoa. He has thought of everything! Packed my bag, got me the day off. But did my colleagues remember, or will I come back to England after the trip of my dreams only to find I have been fired? "They never said anything. Maybe they don't remember. I don't want to lose my job."

"They know. They didn't forget."

"How can you be sure?" Thinking back, I don't see that they acted differently at all. Perhaps they had forgotten.

"Call them. Believe me, they know."

I take out my mobile and dial Janet. "Hi, Janet. Um . . . do you know something I don't?"

Janet is quiet, not wanting to give away a secret. "Well, um . . . perhaps."

"Do you know I'm not coming in to work on Monday?" I ask.

"Oh yes, I know that! Have a fabulous trip! Happy birthday!"

I thank Janet and end the call. Finally it sinks in that we are going to Paris. I have been dreaming of going to Paris since I was a little girl. Even though I am close, living in England, Paris still seems worlds away. But now we are going to Paris. Right. Now.

As my brain gets used to the idea, Ben drops another bomb on me.

"Oh, by the way. We are going first class."

I'm in heaven.

As we drink champagne and discuss the details of Ben's birthday plans for me, I feel like the luckiest girl in the world. I'm sitting across from the most amazing man on earth, who loves me enough to make my biggest childhood dream come true.

Chapter 24

But how do you expect me
To live alone with just me
'Cause my world revolves around you
It's so hard for me to breathe
—"No Air," Jordin Sparks

August 25, 2008

Hey baby,

    We celebrated your birthday yesterday, but I was too upset to write you about it. Leslie and I splurged on afternoon tea at Fortnum and Mason, along with some rose champagne you would have loved. We then wandered around a few of the nicer hotels in the area.

    Outside of the Dorchester, we saw three red Ferraris and one yellow Lamborghini. There was a woman taking a picture of her partner in front of one of the Ferraris. I wish you had been there so I could have taken a picture of you; I know how much you love red Ferraris.

    I so wanted to celebrate your birthday with you. Before you left, I had begun making plans. Remember how I teased you about turning thirty-one? I, of course, was your junior at a mere thirty years old. You kept saying, "I'm still only thirty. I'm still only thirty, Aimee!" I guess you were right.

My plans were for a romantic weekend at the Four Seasons in Canary Wharf. We would have had so much fun. So much alone time together. We led such busy lives that spending time alone together was a treat. It breaks my heart we will never have time alone together again. Now I'm just alone. You are my soul mate, and it's so lonely without you. A huge chunk of my soul is missing.

Thankfully, I had Leslie for a companion on your birthday. We came back to the house after our outing in Central London and opened the bottle of Bollinger we had been saving for a special occasion. We watched Sex and the City *episodes on DVD until well past midnight, in an effort to inspire me to be a single girl again. But I don't want to be single. I want to be with you. Can you see me? Do you hear me? I need you. I thought you needed me too.*

I can feel your presence near me at times, and I feel like you are sending me messages. Like when my fully charged iPod stopped working the other day at the gym just as one of "our songs" started playing on the gym's sound system. Or when I finally gathered up the courage to go back to Richmond Park to run, and I immediately saw a runner with the same build as you and a red running shirt matching the one you so often used to wear. You are everywhere.

Before I woke up on your birthday, I had a dream we were renewing our vows to celebrate your birthday. I was excited to see you and nervous that I wouldn't look nice enough for you. Then I woke up and reality set in.

I know I need to move on, but to say it is difficult is a gross understatement. I want so much to be with you again. I want to hear your voice and feel your touch. I want to fall asleep in your arms and wake up to your smiling face. I miss resting my head on your chest and your soft whispers in my ear. Life without you is not nearly as bright. The sun has vanished, and I'm left to find my way in the darkness.

If only I could sleep forever and find you in my dreams. I love you, Ben. I love you more than these mere words can convey. How about taking me with you? I'd give up everything to be with you again. Remember, I always told you I would die for you. Just so you know, I wasn't kidding! How awesome would it be to be together again? I had always dreamed of being fit and healthy with a positive attitude at eighty-five years old or older. Suddenly that seems like an eternity, and a lonely one at that. Remember how we used to joke that we would race our power scooters when we were old? You had already called the color red, while I chose blue. So, I'll admit it: you probably would have won every race.

I'm ready to be with you when you are ready to have me.

I love you, and I hope you had a great celebration for your birthday yesterday. I hope you and Dad were able to live it up in the afterlife.

Have fun. I love you with all my heart.

> Your soul mate,
> Aimee xoxoxoxoxoxoxo

Chapter 25

It's your birthday
We gonna party like it's your birthday
—"In Da Club," 50 Cent

London, August 2002

How do you top the birthday surprise of being taken on a first-class romantic trip to the place you grew up dreaming about going? Moreover, do it on an intern's budget?

I want to make Ben's birthday as special as he made mine. I am clueless about how I am going to do this. We discuss our finances, and they currently do not include another trip. I must be creative.

Ben is a romantic and I love him. How can I tell him I love him creatively and romantically? I scour the Internet for ideas. Then I find it. Blow up one hundred balloons and fill each one with a message showing how much I love him.

This will be fun. I buy the balloons and think about what to add to them. In one I add a receipt from the first hotel we stayed at together. Other small tokens we have kept thus far in our relationship fill a few others.

What next? I come up with the perfect solution—magnetic poetry! I head to Waterstone's with my colleague Sarah, who is also a big romantic and loves the idea.

"Okay, what have we got here?" she says, looking at the different types of romantic poetry. "Places, romance, erotica." She picks up a box of the erotica version, and I look over her shoulder. We read the examples of included words, and both of us turn beet red. "Okay, maybe not erotica." she says and fumbles the box back on the shelf. "How about romance?"

A little more apprehensively, we look at the examples. They are perfect. "This is going to be great!" Sarah exclaims. I hope I can pull it off and he likes it.

The task is simple. Write just under one hundred poems using the romantic magnetic poetry words. Place them in the rest of the one hundred balloons and blow up said balloons. Oh, and don't let the man you are living with know or see any of what you are doing. This has to be a surprise.

We live in a small two-bedroom flat. Hiding one hundred balloons is a little tricky, to say the least. Luckily, Ben, unlike myself, is not nosy or looking to uncover secrets. When I tell him he cannot go into our spare room for one month before his birthday due to a large surprise waiting for him there, he obliges without question. He's excited for the surprise and doesn't want to spoil it.

Meanwhile, I take time to thoughtfully write poems using the magnets, and then to carefully place one poem in each balloon before blowing it up. This is a little more time-consuming than I expect.

The big day is nearing and I have one hundred filled balloons taking up a large portion of our small second bedroom. All is well. I am ready.

Then a small wrench is thrown in the works.

"Mind if Pauline spends the night?" Ben asks casually during dinner one night. "Her sister is in the hospital in London. I thought she could stay here so it's easier for her to travel there."

Of course this is fine, but what to do with one hundred filled balloons? There is hardly room to walk into the room now, much less sleep. My mind races to find the balloons a new home.

"Sure she can stay. I just need to move your birthday surprise."

I send Ben out to the store and frantically jam one hundred balloons into the small closet space in our main bedroom. I remove some clothes so the balloons can all fit. After some creative maneuvering, I am finally able to close the closet door just as I hear Ben's key in the lock.

I tell him he can no longer look in the closet or open it under any circumstances. He agrees. Our guest comes and goes without Ben sneaking a peek in the closet.

Once the spare room is again free, I transfer the balloons back when Ben isn't home. He can once again take suits and shirts from our closet in the days leading up to his birthday.

The big day arrives, and it's time to move the balloons one final time. I banish Ben to the bedroom as I transfer the balloons to the living room. Pushing together our two love seats, I create an overflowing balloon pit. I have instructed Ben to enter once he hears the music playing. Balloons are *everywhere*. Thank God for small spaces! Our living room has been transformed into a bright, multicolored playground.

I press Play on our stereo, and 50 Cent starts rapping, "Hey Shorty, it's your birthday. We gonna party like it's your birthday." Ben enters the room, and the look on his face is priceless. I immediately know he loves it as much as I loved Paris. When I tell him each balloon is filled with a reason I love him, he loves it even more. He can't believe I fit all the balloons in the closet.

He jumps into the balloon pit. Then we hold hands and both run and jump into the balloon pit. We land in the middle of the love seats and they separate immediately. We land on the floor, laughing hysterically.

We set up the camera and start taking pics to capture the moment. At one point a balloon escapes and floats out the window. Ben runs downstairs and out of the building to retrieve it. He pops a few balloons and loves putting together the poems on our fridge.

We head out to London and have a champagne picnic in the park before going home to play more among the balloons.

Sometimes, it really is the simple things in life that are the most magical.

Chapter 26

London, January 2009

The phone rang a few days before my birthday. My first birthday without Ben. My first birthday without Dad.

It was Alyson, Ben's mum. She asked what my plans were for the day. I had to work for half a day, but I told her I would be home in the early afternoon. We planned a girly day of pampering, I scheduled a beauty therapist to come to the house and give us facials. I was rather excited. This would be fun.

When I arrived home from work Alyson was in the driveway with a bottle of champagne in one hand and a chocolate truffle cake in the other. The woman knew me well. I was grateful to her for making this day special.

We cut the cake and poured the champagne. As we clinked glasses to toast my birthday and dug into the decadence, some potential buyers came to view the house. I had decided to sell. I needed to move on. For the sake of my sanity, I needed to start fresh and create new memories rather than suffocate from the ones that currently surrounded me.

It was a new year. It was time for change. Was I running away from the past or forward towards my future? I didn't know, but I knew I needed to try.

Chapter 27

I plan on being much more than that
And but that's in due time
But until then I'm guilty
And being human's my crime
—"Lil Star," Kelis

Easter 2002

I feel like I'm going to die. Maybe I'll be okay if I just lie perfectly still here in bed without moving a muscle. Forever.

"Are you okay? Feeling any better?" Ben asks from the doorway.

My answer requires movement. As soon as I begin to respond, I'm throwing up again in the bucket next to the bed.

Ben comes up behind me and holds me tight. While I appreciate his concern, it makes my vomiting all the more violent. The more violent it gets, the tighter he squeezes. I don't have the heart to ask him to please stop. He looks on the verge of tears.

I lie back on the bed after the episode finally comes to end. At least for now. Given my track record of the last few hours, I'll be repeating the whole scenario again in twenty minutes.

Ben's concerned eyes look me over. "I've never been so scared in all my life," he tells me.

"I'm so sorry," I apologize once again.

It's Easter weekend. Living and working in England has its perks: the holiday gives you Friday and Monday off from work. I decide to celebrate British-style and make it up to my American girlfriends, whom I ditched to head off to Paris. We hit a few happy hours and, being underpaid interns, make the unwise decision to spend our money on booze and forgo any food.

Before making it to the Tube, we collapse on a park bench and puke profusely. Although I don't remember calling, Ben has seventeen drunken messages on his phone, each one a little more hysterical than the last. Apparently, I call everyone listed in my cell phone that night, begging for a ride home from Covent Garden. I even manage to call my brother, who lives in the United States. Even if he were closer, it would not help much. I am actually in Leicester Square.

Thankfully, we are saved by two kind Australian strangers who pass by and help us. Ben says his heart stopped when he called me after getting all my messages and an unfamiliar voice answered my phone.

If I ever knowingly see these angels again, I will thank them generously for saving my life. Sadly, I will probably never be able to recognize them. I could not open my eyes without puking so they stayed shut for our entire life-saving encounter.

"They gave away our hotel room," Ben says after walking out of our bedroom to make a quick phone call. I don't know what's worse: scaring him to death with my messages; making him drive all the way into Central London to get me; or ruining the romantic weekend in Cornwall we had planned.

Damn it.

He asks if we should cancel the whole thing, but I'm determined to go. We will have this romantic weekend, even if it kills me.

Hours later, the puking continues every twenty minutes like clockwork. We head to see the general practitioner, who gives me a pill to hold off any further heaving.

It works. I'm ready to roll, although feeling fragile.

We drive down to Cornwall, and it's beautiful. We go to St. Michael's Mount and walk around, me rather more slowly than usual.

Then we search for a place to stay. Apparently, Cornwall at Easter is quite popular. Hours go by as we check every single bed and breakfast we pass, finding no vacancies. As it gets dark outside, we go a bit farther afield and out of the way. In what feels like the middle of nowhere, we find a B and B with a single room. The woman will not let both of us stay in the room.

"Sorry. It's against policy," she states.

"But we have nowhere else to stay." We explain.

She gives us a sympathetic look, directed more toward me, as I still look pale and sickly. She tells us if we can't find anything by nine o'clock and she hasn't rented the place, she'll be happy to oblige us then.

We leave and discover this is actually the last place to try without leaving Cornwall. We get some dinner. While I silently pray for the food to stay down, I also ask for no one else to snag this room while we are away.

We return to the B and B and my prayers are answered. We have a small room with one twin bed. Perfect.

As Ben and I lie basically on top of one another in the tiny room, we both let out a laugh. "It's been quite an adventure, hasn't it?" I ask, now feeling human again.

"Yes, Aimee." Ben laughs again. "It was stressful at first, but it's actually been fun. It all worked out in the end. Now I even have a great story to tell about you too." He winks.

Yes. It all works out in the end.

Chapter 28

Is it better now, do you feel like all is fair?
Can we work it out, so it's easier for me to bear?
Because life, it can blind you
—"Can't Let You Go," Matchbox Twenty

London, February 2009

Why wasn't this working? I screamed into the empty air as I threw the cordless phone. It flew through the hallway and landed safely on our bed. I followed it, falling on the bed in despair and screaming loudly into the pillow, which muffled the sound but not my frustration.

The people who had put an offer on our house had withdrawn the offer. This was the second time that had happened. I called the estate agent with whom I had put an offer on a cute apartment overlooking a park. He called me back to tell me it had been sold to someone else.

Every time I felt I was near escaping to a new life, I was drawn back, kicking and screaming, into the old one.

In an effort to calm my frustration, I picked up my notebook and a pen. As the tears flooded down my face, my attack with ink began.

Ben,

I hate you! I hate you! I hate you!!

I hate you for leaving me.

I hate you for leaving me in this house haunted with happy memories.

I hate that I can't sleep in our bed anymore.

I hate that you left me so soon after Dad died.

I hate that you changed my world and shone your light on me, only to leave me to fend for myself in perpetual darkness.

I hate that I get pity stares from everyone who knows and that I'm stuck with your family's grief as well as my own.

I hate that you broke my heart in a million pieces and it will never be the same again.

I hate that you are not working some celestial magic in the afterlife to help me start a new life.

I hate that I'm writing in this notebook that we originally bought together to plan our future and fulfill our hopes and dreams.

With you, life was so easy and effortless. Now nothing is easy. It's fucking ridiculous. I was right from the very beginning.

You are an asshole! Fuck you!

Chapter 29

Now my life doesn't seem so bad
It's the best that I've ever had
Give my love to him finally
—"Finally," Fergie

England to Portugal, 2002

I can't believe how easy and fun life is with Ben. We have snagged a last-minute deal for a week in Portugal. For less than two hundred British pounds (at that time, under three hundred American dollars), we have flights and accommodation for a week in the Algarve.

It's off-season in early spring, but the weather is gorgeous. We lie out by the pool and soak up the sunshine we have been missing in England. In my excitement, I get a bit too much sun and suffer one of the worst burns of my life. But I don't let that stop the fun.

We head off on safari, enjoy the beautiful views up in the mountains, and partake of a local drink known as "fire water," which makes my sunburn seem minimal relative to its heat. We counteract the heat by tasting the local honey. We sign up for a water safari, and it's the first time we see dolphins swimming in the wild. It's beautiful.

We take walks on the beach for hours. It's a little chilly in the morning and evening, and most days we are the only ones there. It feels like we have our own private island. We run up and down the mountains of sand, trying to see who can jump higher, run faster, and go farther. We talk without ever running out of things to say to each other.

The beauty of Portugal is nothing compared to the beauty I see in Ben.

Chapter 30

It's been the longest winter without you
I didn't know where to turn to
See somehow I can't forget you
After all that we've been through
—"Better in Time," Leona Lewis

London, March 16, 2009

Ben,

    I don't hate you. I miss you. My heart hurts without you. Can't believe it has been eight months already. It feels like yesterday we were planning our future. Remember, you were researching for our trip to Turkey? A patient who came in the clinic today is off on a holiday to Turkey, which made me think about that. For months, I couldn't close the Turkey guidebook you had open on our desk, Post-it notes marking pages of hotels and restaurants you found of interest.

    Now I can no longer bear to look at all the pictures I have of us. It seems like a lifetime ago. No; it seems like a different life altogether. Taking down the photos of our life together seemed like the right thing to do.

I packed away our wedding photos. People who visited kept eying them uncomfortably. As they tried to avert their eyes, they were met by my haunted eyes of today, tired and worn from crying day after day—quite the contrast to the happy faces smiling from the frames.

Yesterday was our six-year wedding anniversary, or at least it would have been. Remember how we promised we would celebrate properly this year, as we spent last year at the hospice? So what did I do to celebrate? Thanks for asking. I had reflexology in the morning to help me feel balanced, and your mum and Kevin took me out to Restaurant Noel, our favorite French restaurant.

Some people have commented how strange it must be for me to still live here in our home. Others express how they feel uncomfortable visiting the place, half expecting to see you at any moment. Oddly enough, they never ask how I feel. They are concerned with their own discomfort. They don't know sometimes I fear leaving this place will erase you completely. Other times I want to run away as fast as I can.

I don't know what I want if I can't be with you. Selling the house seemed like the right idea, but it remains on the market with no interest. This limbo state makes me want to run away even more, although I'm not sure where I want to go.

I've decided to use this urge to my benefit. Maybe I can't run away, but I can run. You may be surprised to know that I've been running a lot. I've been training for the marathon in Stratford-upon-Avon. Remember how we promised we would run a marathon together in our thirties? Well, I figured I better get on that. After all, we only have now. If I've learned anything from this whole experience, I have learned that.

So yes, I will be running the marathon, tomorrow! I know you will be with me. I just hope you can keep up! Just kidding. I know you will be running with me in spirit, or at least cheering me on from the sidelines like you always did.

Hope you are having fun wherever you may be. I'm sending you all my love.

Aimee xxx

Chapter 31

To love you when you're right,
Love you when you're wrong
Love you when you're weak,
Love you when you're strong
Take you higher
When the world got you feelin' low.
—"When You Really Love Someone,"
Alicia Keys

London, May 2002

"**O**kay, baby! Are you ready for your first marathon?" I emerge from the bedroom in gray sweatpants and a white T-shirt. Over my T-shirt is a decorated Playtex bra; one cup featuring the American flag while the other has a Union Jack. Glittering silver sequins spell out the words "United We Stand" above the flags. My entrance elicits giggles from my mom and aunt, who are visiting us in London for the week. They have the pleasure of seeing me participate in my first marathon in aid of breast cancer research and awareness. Along with one of the other American interns, we've entered the Playtex Moonwalk, a 26.2-mile, power-walking marathon. The event begins at midnight, and the route takes walkers all around the city: past the London Eye, over Tower Bridge, and ending in Battersea Park. I'm excited.

Ben drops me at the train station and promises to meet me later, as he and my family plan to be cheering amid the crowd near the finish line. Then he drives off to get some sleep before waking up early and driving back to Central London.

My friend and I are among the 15,000 participants power walking that evening. Excitement fills the air among large and small groups of ladies—and a few brave men—dressed in bright pink boas and bras decorated with sequins, feathers, and all sorts of imaginative art. The clock strikes midnight, and we are off.

We start strong, passing many and catching our stride. The lights of London are magical. Whoever thought I would be walking in a decorated bra through the city in the middle of the night, much less with thousands of others? Seeing the surprised looks of the men and women coming out of the bars and nightclubs as we pass is the highlight of whole race.

At around five hours and thirty minutes, our pace is slowing and our energy is waning. We do our best to motivate each other, but the end still seems miles away. One of the other walkers has a radio that is blasting music to help us keep pace. Unable to keep up with him, we fall behind and back into silence.

Desperately thinking of what to do next, I hear a familiar voice calling my name in the distance. "Aimee! *Aimee!*" I turn to my right and am surprised to see Ben. He carries a larger-than-life sign that reads, "Way to go, *Aimee!*" in purple paint, accompanied by stickers of the Union Jack.

No one has ever created a sign for me or cheered me from the sidelines. It warms my heart.

Beside Ben, I see my mom and my aunt, along with Ben's mum and her partner, all clapping and cheering for us as well. Motivated and wanting to be worthy of their praise, we find our second (or third, or fourth) wind and cross the finish line at just over six hours.

Ben's smile meets me at finish line. He passes the sign to my mom and rushes up to hug me and tell me how proud he is of me.

Chapter 32

Head down
As I watch my feet take turns hitting the ground
Eyes shut
I find myself in love racing the Earth
And I'm soaked in your love
And love was right in my path, in my grasp
And me and you belong
—"Smash Into You," Beyoncé

April 26, 2009

I did it, baby! *I completed my first full (running) marathon!* Whoo hoo! *And I came in at three hours, fifty-four minutes, and thirty seconds*—awesome*!*

You were certainly with me every step of the way, I noticed! A black Honda Civic just like yours was parked at the B and B where we stayed, and I instantly knew you were with me!

Then, near the beginning of the race, a person was running rather close right beside me. I didn't want to look over; not sure why, but something kept me from doing so. Once he passed, I watched him from behind, only taking notice because he had been running so close to me. From my vantage point, he looked just like you! Same haircut, same shoulders, same running style. He even held his hands like you did when he ran (yes, I checked you out while running behind you so many times. I know what I'm talking about!).

He ran as fast as you too; I was having trouble keeping up. It was a good thing because I kept running faster in an effort to get closer so I could enjoy the view. Then, suddenly, I was nearly hit by a snot rocket from another runner (gross, I know!). I was shocked and appalled and concentrated on avoiding any further attack. When I was no longer distracted, your lookalike had disappeared. Again, I was left alone.

But when I looked around me, I saw I was surrounded by beauty. The countryside where we ran in Stratford-upon-Avon was stunning—although not quite as stunning as you. You were still with me though. I carried two pictures in my camelback, one of you and me standing with Dad on our wedding day, and one of just you and me.

You make me so happy, even now. I could feel you and Dad pushing me along the course when I got tired. Thank you both.

I love you, gorgeous.
Aimee

Chapter 33

Listen to my heart, can you hear it sings
Telling me to give you everything
Seasons may change winter to spring
But I love you until the end of time
—"Come What May," Moulin Rouge

July 2002

My internship in London is nearing an end. It's been a whirlwind year. We have visited Italy, Portugal, France, Scotland, Wales, and Dublin, as well as having seen various sites in England. We've enjoyed visits from my mom and aunt, my dad and his wife, and my brother. We have celebrated the Queen's Golden Jubilee and watched tennis matches from the stands in Wimbledon. Our love has grown stronger by the day.

But I have this idea in my head that something so wonderful can never last. I also think I'm not good enough for Ben. One day he will wake up and realize he can do a lot better than being with me. Each day he wakes up, though, he seems to love me more. I'm scared I'm going to ruin it or get my heart broken. I'm not sure which is worse.

Once my internship is over, I will technically have to leave the country. Ben and I haven't really discussed what will happen. Ben has started to mention marriage a few times, but I keep brushing him off and changing the subject immediately. Given my parents' history, I'm not thrilled with the thought of getting married. I love this man, but marriage, given what I've seen, is an ending waiting to happen. I don't want this to end. It feels like I'm living in the most glorious dream, and I don't want to wake up.

The other option is for a company in the United Kingdom to sponsor me to stay in the country. It's expensive, and it has to be proven that a British citizen would not be able to be as successful at the job as I am. This seems like a long shot, but I'm hoping I've done well enough where I'm working to at least try.

When I speak to those who have authority in this matter, they tell me it would be great, and much easier, for me to get married, seeing as I'm with someone.

One evening after work, I'm on my way home on the crowded Tube train. I get off a station early and start to walk home, about a twenty-minute journey. Then I have an epiphany. I'm trying to get a job with this company, and I'm not sure if I even want to work there. Why would I do that? Because I want to be with the man that I'm walking home to be with at this moment. I want to be with Ben. I will stay at a job I hate because of him, and limit my choices by doing so. But do I have to do so?

What if we do get married? We love each other. We want to be with each other forever. Isn't that why people get married? I have always seen marriage as an ending because that's all I have ever known. But what if marriage does mean forever? What if it really is "till death do us part"?

I'm five minutes from home, and I know with all my heart I want to spend the rest of my life with Ben. I'm determined to do whatever it takes to be the woman who will make him happy for the rest of his life. This year has been total bliss. I keep thinking it has to come to an end, but does it really? Can we keep it going? What if our entire life is bliss? Can it be possible?

My internal chatter gets louder and louder as I enter the hallway to our apartment. My reason for staying in England would be for Ben. But does Ben want me to stay?

I turn my key in the lock and burst into the apartment with all my thoughts. When I see Ben's beautiful face, my foremost thought pops out of my mouth before I can stop it. "Why haven't you asked me to marry you?" I accuse him.

Looking a little surprised by my outburst, Ben starts to explain. "Well, every time I mention marriage, you change the subject or tell me you don't believe that marriage lasts."

We stare at each other.

"I want to spend the rest of my life with you, Ben," I confess, putting my heart on the line.

Ben's smile lights up his face. "I want to spend the rest of my life with you," he replies.

Our grins get even bigger and we embrace and kiss . . . and kiss. When we come up for air, I look at him questioningly. "So, does this mean we are engaged?"

"Aimee." Ben's blue eyes look deep into mine while we hold each other, lying on our couch. "Let me do this properly."

I look at him, perplexed.

"The ring. The proposal. Let me do it properly. But yes, we are getting married."

We seal the news with a kiss, silly grins plastered to our faces as we embrace on the couch and giggle like school kids. Suddenly all is right in the world, life is good, and I'm happier than I ever imagined possible.

Chapter 34

I know now, just quite how
My life and love might still go on
In your heart and your mind
I'll stay with you for all of time
—"Wherever You Will Go," The Calling

California, June 2009

Dear Ben,

Guess what? I've just had a glimpse of light at the end of this dark tunnel. Remember how you always told me to follow my passions? Well, my passion for food and health has led me to culinary school in Fort Bragg, California, where I'm perfecting the way to make the most delicious and nutritious raw vegan cuisine.

Class began yesterday, and no more than five minutes after walking into the classroom, I had an epiphany. I'm coming home to the States. I feel free here. Free from the reminders that haunt me when surrounded by the things, people, and places where only memories reside. Don't get me wrong. I love our memories, but I need to start fresh. I'll be keeping our memories locked in my head and my heart instead of being forced to look at them in front of my face day after day after day. I feel like I've entered a whole new dimension.

I have yet to decide where in the States I want to reside. My hometown of Detroit is out of the question. Going back to New York would just haunt me more, as we met and fell in love there. California doesn't quite feel right. Maybe Chicago. We only visited there for a short time a few years ago at Christmas, and it's such a great city. Yes, I think that might be it. Watch this space, baby. Soon, your "American Beauty" will be back in America and also be a certified chef! I bet you never thought that would happen, especially remembering how I struggled in the kitchen next to your expertise.

Wow, could it be I am finally getting through the hard times to find a bit of happiness again? The glimmer of hope residing within me is glowing a little brighter.

I wish you every happiness and know you are always with me. Thank you.

Love,
Aimee xxxx

Chapter 35

Moons and Junes and Ferris wheels
The dizzy dancing way you feel
As every fairy tale comes real
I've looked at love that way
—"Both Sides, Now," Joni Mitchell

London, August 2002

It's been weeks since Ben and I decided to get engaged and I promised to let Ben "do it properly." I am not entirely sure what he meant by that but guess it means he will purchase a ring and find a suitable time and place to "surprise" me with a proposal. It seems to be taking a long time. Patience is not one of my strong suits.

After what seems like an eternity, which in reality is probably under three weeks, I turn to Ben before leaving for work.

"I am still waiting."

Ben shakes his head with a smile. He knew this was coming.

"How long can this possibly take?" I ask, wanting to announce to everyone the good news. I have already secretly told a friend and colleague at work . . . well, maybe two . . . or three colleagues. But overall, it is still a secret. One I am eager to share with everyone. I have never been very good at keeping secrets.

"Don't worry, baby," Ben says, not giving away any hints on the possible time and place, leaving me to wonder how much longer I am going to be in suspense.

Then it dawns on me what the plan might be. My dad and his wife are coming to visit next week. Ben is most likely waiting until then so we can all celebrate the good news together. Pleased to know when to expect my surprise, I leave Ben to make his arrangements and promise myself to act surprised for Ben's sake on the day he proposes.

My dad arrives with his wife on August 15, and we arrange to get together with Ben's mum and her partner the next day for dinner. When Ben tells me about the dinner plans, I know that is the moment he will ask. He's going to propose in front of our families.

Now that I know this, I'm free to enjoy the day. The four of us head into Central London to see some sights before the big dinner.

Our first stop is the London Eye, an enormous Ferris wheel. I'm surprised my stepmother agrees to go on, as she has a fear of heights. She assures me she is fine and really wants to see the view of the city. I look up at the Eye and miss my dad and Ben making a quick exchange.

When we get to the front of the line twenty minutes later, we board a capsule along with about fifteen other tourists. As we begin our ascent, we chat about how beautiful the day is, bright and clear. Ben points out the main sights to my parents.

Just before the capsule reaches its highest point, Ben grabs my hand. While everyone gathers to one side to enjoy the view of Big Ben and the Houses of Parliament, Ben pulls me to the back of the capsule. He pulls me with such force that I lose my footing and knock into the side of the capsule. As I regain my balance, Ben keeps pulling me away from everyone else.

"You need to sit down," he says urgently.

"Are you okay?" I ask. He is sweating and looks a bit pale.

"Sit down!" he says again, and I immediately oblige.

He bends down on one knee. I'm still thinking he is not feeling well when I see him take a small box out of his pocket. He takes my hand. "Aimee. When I'm with you, I'm on top of the world. So I wanted to literally be on top of the world when I asked you to be my wife."

Tears start to stream down my face. It really is a surprise, and totally worth the wait.

He opens the box to reveal the most beautiful diamond ring I have ever seen in my life. I find out later he has been researching diamonds for the past few weeks and has chosen one that is nearly flawless. He removes the ring from the box as I hold out my hand. When he places it on my finger, we look at each other with surprise. It fits perfectly.

My dad snaps a picture of the moment. The other people in the pod are all focused on the sights. No one has noticed this monumental moment except one little girl, who puts her hand over her mouth as she lets out a squeal of surprise.

We exit the London Eye an engaged couple. It's time for a celebration, and we head to the nearest pub for some bubbly and lunch. After a toast, Ben reveals how he took on the second job of becoming a diamond expert in the last few weeks and all the effort that went in to picking the perfect ring. I'm impressed. It is perfect.

Ben and Dad relate the phone conversation they had when Ben called to ask for my hand. I can't believe I had no idea all this was going on. Maybe I would have been more patient during the last two weeks if I had known. Maybe not.

We discuss plans for our upcoming nuptials. April is the month decided upon.

Later that evening, we meet Ben's mum and her partner. Having chosen the month for our big day, I say to her without thinking that we have a big surprise for her coming in about nine months. She nearly faints.

We clear up the confusion and are soon popping open another bottle of champagne to celebrate our engagement. Being surrounded by the people I love so dearly—Ben, my dad, Ben's mum, and her partner Kevin—I can't imagine life getting any better. It's just like the engagement ring. It's perfect.

Chapter 36

I'll never leave you behind
Or treat you unkind
I know you understand
And with a tear in my eye
Give me the sweetest goodbye
That I ever did receive
—"Sweetest Goodbye," Maroon 5

London, July 4, 2009

I was back from culinary school and busy in the kitchen, preparing a meal that I hoped would impress my in-laws. Alyson and Kevin had come over for a meal so they could check out my new skills while we caught up. I promised it would be delicious, and I hoped and prayed they liked it.

I had spent the week going over menus of what they might like best, and settled on raw vegan enchiladas, salad, salsa, and guacamole. Mexican food had been Ben's favorite, and I wondered if he would have enjoyed the meal too. For dessert, I made cheesecake, one of Alyson's favorites—if the raw vegan version is up to scratch.

But it wasn't only the food I was worried about. I would also be sharing with them my decision to leave England, and I was unsure what their reactions would be. Whatever those reactions were, I knew in my heart I was making the right decision for me.

Quite fittingly, it was the Fourth of July—Independence Day in America. I couldn't have thought of a better day to declare my own independence.

They arrived, and we exchanged stories about the goings-on of life during the previous month. I showed them my new contraption, a nine-tray Excalibur dehydrator. They looked a little apprehensive about the food. When we sat down at the table in the conservatory, they eyed their plates suspiciously and exchanged a glance when they thought I wasn't looking. "Enchiladas that are not cooked? How is that again?"

After another brief explanation of the method and the benefits, they lifted their forks for the first bite. A look of surprise came over both of them, followed by smiles. Soon the large plates of food in front of them were clean, and Kevin asked for a second helping.

Pleased by my success, I served up dessert and prepared myself. When I told them I had some big news to share, they looked at each other the same way they had before I announced my engagement to Ben. "You're not pregnant, are you?" Alyson asked, and we all laughed at the ridiculous question. It broke the serious mood hanging over us. They knew what was coming, and I confirmed it by announcing my decision to move back stateside.

They were happy for me and supported my decision. Sadness showed in their eyes but not their actions. I cleared the dessert plates, now empty, and put the kettle on for three cups of tea.

Chapter 37

You love me, you complete me
You hold my heart in your hands
And it's okay 'cause I trust that
You'll be the best man that you can
—"You Complete Me," Keyshia Cole

London to Richmond, Virginia, October 2002

I'm leaving the United Kingdom. Ben and I have discussed it, and this short-term plan seems the best. My internship ended in September, along with my student visa. Although I am permitted to stay in the country with a fiancée visa, it is illegal for me to be employed until after we are married. With only Ben's salary, we can't make ends meet. It's barely enough for his own needs, and we are by no means living an extravagant life.

My dad tells me I can move back home and work at his pharmacy. My brother, who lives in Virginia, insists I come stay with him. The thought of living in a new city is more appealing than going back to Michigan, so I take my brother up on his offer and book my ticket to Richmond.

Ben and I stand just outside the security entrance at Heathrow Airport. We won't see each other again until just before Christmas. He has packed his Tigger in my suitcase, a worn-out stuffed animal that his grandmother made for him when he was a baby. He says it will keep me company while we are apart. I know the animal holds a lot of sentimental value for Ben, and I am touched he has entrusted me with it.

For the past month I have been working on my gift to Ben. I want it to be just as special and sentimental. I want him to know I will be thinking about him every day. I want to show him how much I truly love him and feel like the luckiest girl in the world to be his fiancée.

For each day of the initial two and a half months we will be apart (until Ben comes to visit in Michigan for Christmas with my family), I place a picture we took together, along with a note. Each note has a date clearly written on it. On the designated day, Ben will open the note to find something special: a poem, a love letter, a memory, a shared dream. Each day he will read some written token of my affection for him while I am miles away, missing him. The gift is waiting to surprise him when he arrives home.

Little do I know that while I am away, Ben will be working on his own photo book, detailing our love story. He will present it to me for a wedding gift. The book is filled with pictures and stories, including being separated by an ocean during our engagement. One page, in large, multicolored letters (each cut out separately from a magazine), reads, "The hardest times." On that page, he writes in silver ink:

> *The best gifts are those that come from the heart, and your book of photos and daily notes really kept me going through the hard times. It was one of the best presents I have ever received.*
>
> *Being apart from you is the hardest thing in the world. It is like all the fun, happiness, and love has just been sucked out of the air, and I feel lost . . .*
>
> *Yet I continuously remind myself that I am still the luckiest man alive because I have found "the one"—that person that you*

know you have to be with, that person who brings out the best in you. Makes you feel emotions again. The person who lights up your world when you hear her voice or see her in the street. You feel tingly inside when she touches you or even just looks at you and smiles. The one who makes you feel complete; the missing piece of the jigsaw that makes who you are.

Aimee, I miss you so much it hurts, and I am so thankful that I have found true love with you.

Chapter 38

Has the fear taken over you?
Tell me
Is that what you want
To make up your life?
—"My, My, My," Rob Thomas

London, July 16, 2009

I t had been a year. I couldn't believe it.

An entire year had passed since that insistent knock on my door. Had I known that opening the door would be the end of my beloved reality, whisking me into my worst nightmare, I surely would not have opened it.

It was my last day working at the clinic. When I made the decision to leave London, I had put in my notice and realized my last day would coincide with the anniversary of Ben's death. As I sat at the front desk for the last time, I felt like a complete failure.

My mind drifted back to when I originally got the job. I had left my role as client service manager at a company in Central London because I was bored and frustrated. I knew I had more to offer. Ben supported me in my decision as I tried to discover a career that would ignite my passion.

Six months passed, and my passion was still playing hide-and-seek. One day, out of the blue, I got a call from someone I had met in town. She told me there was an opening at a local chiropractic clinic. The thought of walking to work and avoiding the daily commute on the Tube was enough to get me to apply. When I discovered it paid relatively well and involved some travel to Europe, I got excited and seriously started to consider it an option.

When I told Ben, he warned me not to take a job that was mainly administrative. "It's not utilizing your many talents, Aimee. They'll be wasted in an admin job, and you'll get bored quickly." We discussed the pros and cons and made a decision. I would take the job, but we agreed it was only temporary. I promised to leave in two years, if not before, to pursue my passions and utilize my skills fully.

And now I sat, bored, on my final day at work, three years after the promise was made.

In my mind, I kept making excuses for why it took me an extra year. Well, the man I made the promise to died; clearly I had to recoup. I needed something familiar around me while my whole world was turned upside down. I did go part time after two years—didn't that count? In fact, as the weight of the broken promise got heavier with time, I continued to cut my hours. But it took me a whole year to cut the cord completely.

Why? Because I was scared. Of what? Rejection? Failure? My two biggest fears had become a reality in the last year. What was I waiting for?

The two people closest to me had died, and I was still afraid to live.

Chapter 39

Boy I hear you in my dreams
I feel your whisper across the sea
I keep you with me in my heart
You make it easier when life gets hard
—"Lucky," Jason Mraz

Richmond, VA, October-November 2002

I have become what I most hate: aimless and engrossed in television. This is not what I expected.

When I arrive in Richmond, I discover how often my brother travels for work. He is gone for weeks at a time. Finding temporary work is much more difficult than I anticipated. I often find myself at home, alone, in front of the television.

Ben and I arrange to talk every two to three days. He uses a prepaid phone card, and our conversations are kept short to save money. After expressing how much we miss each other, the topic often turns to the plans for our wedding and honeymoon. We had hoped to visit Australia for our honeymoon—a trip that seems more expensive by the day, given our current financial status.

I tell Ben that the honeymoon can wait or we can go elsewhere, on a more budget-friendly honeymoon. But Ben is convinced it should be Australia. Until one day.

"So, Aimee. I have been thinking."

"I thought I smelled smoke through the phone," I joke.

"Ha ha. Seriously, I've given Australia a lot of thought, and I really want to spend our honeymoon there."

"I know you do."

"Well, I want our honeymoon to be really special. But I think it might be a bit out of our price range. So I am thinking maybe we can go somewhere else and postpone Australia until the next year. We'll go for our anniversary."

"Sounds good to me. Oprah says the first year of marriage is the hardest, and that most break up over financial issues and overspending. So it's good to avoid that."

There is silence on the line. I've just outed myself as a television junkie.

"Did you just say 'Oprah says that'?" Ben asks incredulously.

"Well, umm, it was what I was thinking, and I'm just saying it was reinforced by *The Oprah Winfrey Show.*"

"I see. I didn't realize you watched *The Oprah Winfrey Show.* What else does Oprah say? Are we still allowed to get married?" He is playing with me now. I hear the laughter in his voice.

"Ha ha. Life isn't easy without you. I'm reduced to sitting in front of the television while I wait for your call."

"Well, I shall call you again on Thursday. Any other shows you are watching that I should know about?"

Before I take time to think about it, I blurt out another confession. "Well, if you could call about nine o'clock your time instead of eight, that would be great. *General Hospital* comes on at three o'clock my time, and there is a guy on it who reminds me of you. So, when he is on the show, I feel like I'm spending time with you."

There is more silence on the line before Ben asks in stunted words, slowly, "Are. You. Serious?"

I want to say no, but I can't do it. I really do feel closer to him while I watch his lookalike on TV. "Well . . ."

"Oh, honey. We need to get you out of there. I will call you Thursday. Try to keep some grasp on your sanity until then. I love you."

He is right. I'm going a little crazy without him. I tell him I love him too, and we hang up. I am already looking forward to his call on Thursday—and hoping it is at nine o'clock instead of eight.

Chapter 40

I couldn't turn on the TV
Without something there to remind me
—"Better in Time," Leona Lewis

London, July 2009

I sat in front of the television, eating lunch. My plate of mixed vegetable salad and flax crackers rested on my lap as I watched reruns of *The Gilmore Girls*. Ben was gone, but I was still trying to be with him by finding his doppelgängers on television. There was a character on that show that reminded me of him.

Interestingly enough, as the show's seasons progressed, the lookalike character's hairstyle evolved the same way Ben's had, from spiky to short. While logically you could argue it was due to time and the changing popularity of certain styles, I liked to think Ben was sending me a message from beyond. Though I couldn't help but think Ben would probably be disappointed with my pathetic attempts to be united with him again.

My fruitless search didn't stop at the television. The previous week, I had gone to a church that hosted a medium, who was channeling the spirits of those who had crossed over. On the way there, I got lost and frustrated. Upset that I would be late, I began telling off Ben in my mind. How dare he leave me here! How dare he! And now to send me in the wrong direction! Yes, it was all his fault. I projected all my pain and suffering onto his spirit, in hopes he would show up to defend himself.

But Ben was never a fighter. Whenever I got irritated or angry at the world, Ben would calmly tell me that he was not going to speak to me until I was my happy self again.

When I finally did arrive at the church, ten minutes late, I found the medium had not shown up. Everyone waited until someone came to tell us she had canceled. Thanks, Ben. I got your message loud and clear. I'll be my happy self when I return.

When I returned to the church weeks later, Ben still didn't make an appearance through the medium. I figured he probably had better things to do with his time now.

Oddly enough, about a month later I got a call from an energy healer who wanted to offer his services for the breast cancer charity group that I ran with a friend. I was intrigued. We set up a small event in my friend's living room and invited people to hear him talk about energy healing and how he could apparently talk to the dead.

He did not know I was widowed. Given what he told us about himself, I was amazed he didn't pick up this tidbit of information. To me, it felt like the word *widow* was etched into my forehead for all to see, and should have glowed in neon for those who could see the beyond.

Finally, my friend could no longer stand it and told him of my loss. She asked him point-blank if he could speak to Ben. The healer looked at me in utter shock. At that moment, I could see in his eyes that he was a fraud.

I was so desperate to talk to Ben that I pushed this knowledge out of my mind and pretended that what the healer was saying was true. But the lies only became more apparent. He referred to Ben as "Benjamin." Ben was named simply Ben; "Ben" was not short for anything, and Ben was *always* quick to point this out. He would never have told someone his name was Benjamin.

The healer went on to relate nothing of substance. He shared ambiguous information that could have applied to any human being who once walked the earth. I was devastated and stayed silent to hide my disgust.

When the man finally left, he told me, "Ben is saying he wants you to hug me."

I knew Ben very well. And I knew for a fact that he would at this point have wanted me to punch this fraud in the face. But I also knew he liked me best when I was calm and cool. So I put on my most stunning fake smile and thanked the man for his time.

Chapter 41

I wanna send this one out to my vanilla ice-
cream chocolate pudding pie
That stayed with me in the hood, do or die
—"Take Me As I Am," Wyclef Jean featuring Sharissa

Virginia to Michigan, December 24, 2002

I am trying to play it cool, but I am anxious to see Ben. It is 5:30 a.m. and we will soon be on our way to Michigan. But not soon enough for me. We have been delayed a few days because of my brother's work schedule.

My gift of daily love notes and pictures to Ben ended the day he got on the plane from London to Detroit. I quickly put together a few more letters and pictures and send them to him in the mail, so my love notes are uninterrupted until I see him, according to my original plan. When I speak to him, he says it is strange being at my dad's home without me, but they are enjoying Christmas shopping together.

"I was looking for a T-shirt to commemorate my time here on the mean streets of Detroit without you. I thought I'd be able to find one saying, in dripping red letters, 'I survived Detroit,' accompanied by some fake bullet holes."

"Well, who is the crazy one now?" I ask.

He laughs and passes the phone to my dad, who isn't a fan of shopping. He tells me he is astounded that Ben spent hours searching every store for the perfect winter hat, only to go back to the very first store they visited to buy the first one he saw. I hear Ben laughing in the background before he gets back on the phone. He tells me how amusing it is to watch Dad shop for clothes for his wife, and how Dad bought the same sweater in seven different colors.

They get along really well, even though they don't quite understand each other's quirky habits. One thing they can agree on is ice cream, and they end the call in order to go get some.

Now I'm in the car, wrapped up warm and ready to go. My brother goes to check the house one more time to make sure everything is in order and all electrical items are shut off. After two minutes of eternal waiting, I slam on the car horn, not caring about waking up the neighbors. His figure appears at the door. He flips me the bird and goes back inside. I vow to take back his Christmas gift if he's not out within five minutes. He makes it just in time, and we are finally on the road.

When we make it to my dad's house in Michigan, it is nearly seven o'clock. As we pull into the familiar driveway, I'm deliriously happy, bouncing up and down on my seat, much to my brother's dismay. As soon as the car stops, I leap out.

I see my two best friends in the world come to greet me on the porch. I hug Dad first, knowing that when I put my arms around Ben, I will never let go. Dad always gives the best hugs, squeezing me so tightly I can barely breathe.

My eyes then lock with Ben's. We stare at each other for a moment, not believing this is real, that we are finally together again. We embrace and kiss, and everything in the world is once again right.

We get our bags and head into the house. Dad offers us drinks. As he prepares them, Ben and I poke each other on the shoulder to make sure the other is real.

"This feels too good to be true." Ben says.

I agree. Feels like we are in a dream. Best Christmas yet.

Chapter 42

What an amazing time
What a family
How did the years go by?
Now it's only me
—"What You Waiting For,"
Gwen Stefani

London, July 2009

I n five short months, it would be my second Christmas
without Ben. Without my dad. It was still hard to believe.
Life no longer felt real. I wondered if it ever would again.

My thoughts drifted back to last Christmas. I flew into Dulles
International Airport from London, having accepted an invitation
to spend Christmas in Virginia with my brother and his wife. I
appreciated how they had been there for me since Ben's death.

My brother picked me up. The traffic from DC to Richmond
was worse than normal. What should have taken about two hours
ended up taking five. Halfway through, we stopped for a bite to
eat. He jokingly asked if I would eat at a burger joint, knowing
my diet was mainly vegetarian and very healthy.

To his astonishment, I accepted the challenge and, for the first
time in a very long time, dined on a burger and fries. Two days

later I was violently ill, my digestive system not knowing how to handle what I had put in my body. I lay, curled in the fetal position on their bathroom floor for hours in agony, while my sister-in-law tried to alleviate the damage by making me green juice.

The next day their house flooded when a pipe burst, and we were all out. The floors were taken up and industrial fans placed throughout the damaged areas. They ran at a high speed constantly, giving all of us headaches. The dust and debris brought up left me with the worst head cold I have had in my life. One day I slept for sixteen hours straight without moving an inch.

When I was well enough to move again, I got an e-mail from neighbors in England, who told me my shed had been broken into and quite possibly my house. I dissolved in tears.

We went out to eat, as there was no way we could eat at home with the floors taken up, and the lights went out in the restaurant, leaving us in darkness for the entire meal.

On Christmas Eve, I opened their Christmas card to me and thought they had made a mistake when I saw it was addressed to "Aunt Aimee." A moment later, I realized it was "Aunt-to-be." They announced that their first baby was due in August. I was ecstatic.

We bid good riddance to 2008 and I braced myself for blessings in 2009.

Chapter 43

Is this a dream?
If it is
Please don't wake me from this high
I'd become comfortably numb
Until you opened up my eyes
To what it's like
When everything's right
—"You Found Me," Kelly Clarkson

Michigan, December 2002

"They are having a baby."

"What? Seriously?"

Ben is filling me in on what's been going on since my absence. I'm surprised to learn his dad and stepmom are expecting.

"Wow. I didn't see that coming. That's fantastic!"

"Ah, but there's more great news, Aimee! We won!"

"Won what?"

"The bet. We won it!"

"We did? I knew it!"

"The bet" had been made between me and Ben and his mum and her partner. Each pair bet the other would get married first, both couples claiming they would never get married. When Ben and I announced our engagement to Alyson and Kevin, we had also announced our defeat. Little did we know they too were already engaged and keeping it quiet from everyone. I'm impressed they kept the secret so long. I certainly would have struggled to stay quiet about our engagement. I tell complete strangers that we are engaged.

"When is the wedding?"

"Mum's fiftieth birthday. She'll find any excuse to keep people from noticing it," Ben says jokingly.

My heart sinks at the date. Her birthday is in January, and I'll still be living stateside. I can't believe I'll miss such a big event.

Ben sees the look of despair cross my face. "Don't worry," he assures me. "You are going to be there."

"I am?"

"You are. Mum and Kevin paid for your flight. You are coming back for their wedding. They wouldn't have you miss it, after all. We did win the bet; it's the least they can do," Ben says with a wink.

"*Yay!* I'm so excited! Oh! I need to buy a dress. What will I wear? Where is it they are getting married? What is your mum wearing? Where is the reception? How long am I in England?"

The questions keep coming and Ben answers them all. Making it all even better, I'll be staying there a week, so I can spend my own birthday with Ben in London.

Life is full of exciting surprises.

Chapter 44

Man gave names to all the animals
In the beginning, in the beginning
Man gave names to all the animals
In the beginning, long time ago.
—"Man Gave Names to All of the Animals,"
Bob Dylan

London to Richmond, VA, July 2009

"It's going to be a surprise. You'll have to wait."

"Just tell me! I won't tell anyone! I promise." I had been trying to get my brother to reveal the name of the baby, who, I was delighted to discover, is a girl. Now I needed to know this little girl's name.

"You'll just have to call her Princess Pork Chop until she arrives," I heard my sister-in-law say in the background.

"Well, if I refer to her as Princess Pork Chop for nearly nine months, the name is going to stick once she's here. She'll be known as Princess Pork Chop to me forever, and you'll have to live with the consequences of her hating you for it."

"Fine, Aimee. We will live with it." He hung up, and I was left to wonder.

"A romantic surprise birthday trip to Paris.
Can you see the Eiffel Tower hiding in the clouds?"

"Jumping into the birthday balloon pit I created for
Ben. Look closely and you will see his legs!"

"Dad walking me down the aisle to
Ben on our wedding day."

"Our perfect wedding day."

"Our belated honeymoon in Australia."

"Moving into our home in Hounslow!"

"Emotions fly high with the gift of a glider trip for Ben's birthday."

"Ben cooking up a feast on our last Christmas together."

"A magical trip to Iceland."

"The last photo taken of us together. On
the beach near Bamburgh Castle."

Chapter 45

Oh, come what may, come what may
I will love you, oh I will love you
Suddenly the world seems such a perfect place
—"Come What May," Moulin Rouge

London, January 2003

"I love you so much. I just couldn't live without you."

It's my birthday, and Ben and I are celebrating at our home, a small, two-bedroom apartment in Isleworth. I can't think of a better birthday gift than just being with Ben. I feel like the luckiest girl in the world when he tells me those words.

His mum's wedding was fantastic, and the happy couple was not at all concerned about losing the bet. The sun shone brightly the whole day, mirroring their radiant faces. It was such a privilege to be witness to such an extraordinary day. I am excited for our wedding day to approach, although it doesn't seem like it will come fast enough. Tomorrow I will be on a plane back to the States for another two months. It feels like an eternity.

When I do get back to Virginia, I'm surfing the Web and come across a site full of questions couples should ask each other before committing to marriage. I think asking a question via e-mail each day will help Ben and I feel closer and enable us to learn even more about each other. Ben agrees, and so the fun begins.

Some questions are silly, while others are more serious. I write the question each day and send it to Ben, putting my answer after a generous amount of space so Ben will not see it until he has his answer ready. He then e-mails me his answer.

February 3, 2003

Okay, here is the second question of the day—bit of a tricky one:

What five things have you done in your life that you are most proud of?

My answer:
In chronological order, here goes:

1. *Moved to NYC*
2. *Graduated from college with honors*
3. *Overcame shyness (well, pretty much!)*
4. *Moved to England*
5. *Marrying the man of my dreams (couldn't have done it without you, baby!)*

Mostly, I'm just proud of you and impressed that you want to be my husband! I'll do everything in my power to be the best wife to you a man ever had. :)

Lots of love,
Aimee

Hey girl!
Here are my answers:

— *Completing AIDSRide*
— *Graduating from university*
— *Seeing my mum get married*
— *Actually going to NYC*
   And, finally,
— *Proposing to you and getting you to say yes (after a little kiss!)*

Love,
Ben XOXO

February 18, 2003

Hey baby!
   Hope you had fun last night at your dinner.

Here is the question of the day:

Over the last five years, how do you think you have changed for the worse? Better?

My answer:

Hmm . . . I think I have changed for the better by being calmer in the last five years. Well, more like the last two years, really . . . :) I have learned how to take things less seriously, just have fun, and enjoy life.

Love you,
Aimee
xoxo

Hey baby,

The dinner was good. Long day though; got home and went to bed!

Out again tonight! Will call you tomorrow, baby!

Answer:

Without a doubt I think I have changed for the better. I have become a little less shy and have accepted who I am and being an individual, rather than trying to fit in. Most importantly though, I have found true love and have been shown how to love and be loved in return.

I love you . . .
Ben XOXOXO

Chapter 46

My yesterdays are all boxed up and neatly put away
—"Always on Your Side," Sheryl Crow

London, September 2009

I 'd begun sorting through everything in the house so I could
ascertain what I wanted to send to the States when the time
for the big move arrived. Standing at the built-in bookshelves
in our room, I began to take the contents off the bottom shelf.
Our photo albums were all lined up, and I couldn't help but open
up our wedding album and the one containing pictures of our
beautiful honeymoon together.

Next to the photo albums stood a white binder. I pulled it
out and saw it was a training manual that Ben received at work. I
wondered why he kept it next to our precious memories.

As I flipped through the binder, I realized it was a self-
development course Ben's company provided in 2004. Being a life
coach, I was intrigued to see what the course contained. One page
had Ben's familiar handwriting on it. I paused, running my hands
gently over the letters. I was reminded of the many handwritten
notes Ben left me during our years together: "I love you," or "You're
the best." Notes that expressed "good luck" when I was going to a
job interview or "I miss you" when he was traveling for work.

His words on this particular piece of paper were answers to a printed question that read, "What are your goals for the next five years?"

Ben's answers:

- Buy a house
- Get promoted within the company
- Travel extensively
- Be the best husband I can possibly be

By the time my eyes took in the last line, my heart hurt and tears were pouring from my eyes. I was so grateful that Ben had achieved all these goals. He was such an amazing man and truly the best husband from the very beginning. Mine were tears of happiness that he had done what he set out to do. And tears of sadness for the many goals he created after this but never had the chance to fulfill.

As my body began to shake with sobs, I realized how grateful I was that the tables had not been turned. Being the one left behind was much harder, and the pain, although dulled at times, never went away. I was grateful I could spare Ben the pain of losing me. It was something I would not have wished on my greatest enemy, much less my best friend.

*I will take the pain for you, Ben. It's the least I can do. And
I will prove to you I can get through this and make you proud.*

Chapter 47

It's this 1 thing that caught me slippin'
It's this 1 thing I want to admit it
This 1 thing and I was so with it
It's this 1 thing you did
—"1 Thing," Amerie

London 2005

"You know what I love about you the most? And don't take this the wrong way and get mad at me for saying this."

Oh no, I thought. "Go ahead."

"Well, it's kinda weird, but it's true. Of course you are beautiful and sexy and fun and smart and . . ."

"Ben," I cut him off, "just tell me!"

"Well, what I love about you the most is . . . you are . . . *adaptable*."

"What?"

"You're adaptable. It's pretty amazing. You can go into any situation and thrive. It's impressive."

"Hmmm . . ." I am thinking I like smart and sexy better. I don't really understand what he means about being adaptable.

Ben senses this and goes on to explain. "Like in New York, then London. Or really any given situation. You make it wherever you are and whatever you are doing. You make friends so easily anywhere and everywhere you go. Good friends. I find it a lot harder, so you impress me. And it's the thing I love most about you."

I think about this for a moment. I guess I can see his point. "But you make friends easily too. You thrive in different situations too."

"Not like you. You could be put anywhere, through anything, and you would come out on top."

Before I can give it any more thought, Ben wraps his arms around me, his blue eyes penetrating deeply into my own.

"Did I mention you are beautiful and sexy too?" he asks before kissing me.

Chapter 48

But is there someplace far away, someplace where all is clear
Easy to start over with the ones you hold so dear
Or are you left to wonder, all alone, eternally
This isn't how it's really meant to be
No, it isn't how it's really meant to be
—"Always By Your Side," Sheryl Crow

London, September 2009

I made the decision to rent the house instead of selling. Once I had a tenant, I would be ready to go.

Sorting out the belongings we had accumulated over the years was not an easy task. I spent hours on my own, clearing out the attic while I thought about how scared I had been to even go up in the attic while Ben was still here. It was funny how, when things needed to be done, you stepped up and did them and left your fear behind.

Friends and family helped me by taking me to car boot sales, where I could pass on things I no longer needed, like DVDs, books, and Ben's old rollerblades that he hadn't used since living in New York. We'd always had the intention of going rollerblading together . . . one day.

I passed many items to his family that I felt might be of use or of sentimental value to them. To his dad, I gave a signed Jenson

Button shirt and framed photo that Ben had been excited to own. His dad was another racing enthusiast.

Dishes and cutlery went to Ben's sister, who was moving into her first apartment. His favorite leather jacket went to his brother. His cookbook collection and knife set went to his stepdad, who was an avid cook. Video games went to his younger brothers, much to their delight. I did the best I could to fulfill what Ben would have wanted. Most of all, I knew he would have wanted all of us to be happy.

I sold the electrical products, like my high-speed blender, juicer, and dehydrator. They wouldn't work in the States. The money I got for them would go toward buying the same products when I got home.

Items I couldn't sell, I gave to charity. A friend of mine picked up a carload of items for her charitable rummage sale. She went off with Ben's colorful sneakers peeking out from a bag and his extra motorcycle gear. Larger items, like the television and the futon I had rested on for all those sleepless nights, were loaded into vans for the local charity shop.

With every item that left the house, I felt lighter. Freer. Space was opening up for my new life to grow. While at times I was sad, I tried to focus more on the adventure and what lay ahead. Whatever happened, Ben's spirit would always remain in my heart.

Over the years, we had kept every card, note, and picture we took. There were an incredible number of photographs. Although I wanted to always keep those, I felt I could not take them with me during my attempt to create a new life. It would be like having a photo of a beautifully decadent chocolate cake before your eyes after you've vowed never to eat chocolate again. It was dooming myself to failure.

Alyson came to the rescue and offered space in her loft for me to store the precious reminders of my love story with Ben. Boxes and boxes, eight years' worth of birthday and anniversary cards, love notes, and photos, were packed into her car. She carefully carried out the last item: a large bag containing my beautiful wedding dress.

Chapter 49

At long last love has arrived
And I thank God I'm alive
—"Too Good to Be True," Lauren Hill

England, April 24, 2003

"Wow. You are beautiful."
I hear my dad's words as he steps inside the bridal suite. He is ready to do his duty and walk me down the aisle.

The day has finally come. Our wedding day. We will never have to be apart again.

It hasn't been easy, but we have made it. I want to look spectacular for Ben, to be worthy of being his wife.

The wedding dress is one I have searched for in many shops with Alyson. When I have all but given up hope, we come across a bridal shop in Farnborough. We go inside with high hopes but low expectations. The shop assistant looks me over and immediately picks out an array of white dresses for me to try on. When she chooses a strapless dress with lots of sparkles, Alyson and I exchange a look of distaste. The assistant sees this but insists I try it on anyway. She assures us it will look different once on. I follow her as she carries the dresses off to the fitting room.

I save the distasteful dress for last, thinking I'll like the others better, but nothing seems quite right. Begrudgingly, I try on the sparkly, strapless dress and look at myself in the mirror.

I'm in shock. The sequins twinkle in the light and I finally feel like a bride. This is the one.

When I step out of the dressing room to show Ben's mum and his sister, tears well up in Alyson's eyes. This has not happened with any of the other multitude of dresses I have tried on. All three of us agree it is indeed the one.

Now, as I look at myself in the dress on my wedding day, life feels surreal. Never have I been this happy before. I'm grateful my dad is here. Surrounded by the people I love most in the world, Dad and I walk arm in arm down the aisle. Ben turns, catching his breath at the first sight of his bride.

Huge smiles stay on our faces the entire ceremony. When it is time to exchange rings, I keep saying, "Left, left, left" in my head so I will place Ben's ring on the correct finger.

Ben places the band on my left ring finger. Then he holds up his right hand, which confuses my inner mantra. We stop and look at each other. Ben quickly puts down his right hand and holds up his left.

The crowd gives a little laugh, and I put Ben's custom-made platinum wedding band on the correct ring finger. We giggle at each other. Is this real?

And then it happens:

We are pronounced husband and wife.

Chapter 50

And when the worrying starts to hurt
And the world feels like graves of dirt
Just close your eyes until
You can imagine this place, yeah, our secret space at will
—"Shut Your Eyes," Snow Patrol

London-Devon, September 2009

I sat staring at a picture from our wedding day. Dad was on my right while Ben stood on my left. We were all smiling outside the one-hundred-year old house where we had just had the ceremony. It was one of the happiest days of my life. If someone had told me that, five short years later, I would be the only one in the picture still on this earth; I would not have believed it in a million years.

Although I had packed up most of our pictures to store in Alyson's loft, I couldn't help but save a few to carry as a reminder that it hadn't been a dream. I really had been part of a fairy tale. Well, maybe except for that "happily ever after" bit.

The house had been through a detox with all the clearing and decluttering I had done, and I felt my body needed to follow suit. Before leaving the United Kingdom, I looked up some detox retreats I could attend in an effort to clear some emotions and create space for my new life. I felt there was a happily-ever-after ending in my future if I went for it, although it couldn't be what I had expected. I had no idea what it would look like, but I felt it necessary to try. After all, I thought, I must still be here for a reason. Everything had a purpose, after all. What was mine?

I asked around, and the recommendation for a retreat in Devon came up more than once. I checked out their Web site and saw the next retreat was at the end of September, a few short weeks away. I was planning to leave in October, so the timing was perfect.

The Web site said they had two spots left, but when I tried to book using their online form, I kept getting rejected. I picked up the phone to book directly but got their answering service, which stated there was now only one spot. I left my message and contact details. A few hours later, I got a call back with bad news. The retreat was fully booked for September. Did I want to book October?

Although I didn't have a tenant for my house yet, I was determined to leave in October. I had set the intention, declaring to the powers that be, that the perfect tenant would come any day now, allowing me to depart. I explained to the retreat organizer that I was leaving the country and had to have the September date. "Thanks so much for calling me back. I guess this just wasn't meant to be." I wondered how many times I would go down roads that seemed perfect, but would later find "weren't meant to be." I wondered what *was* meant to be, and asked whatever power/energy/universe/god there was to maybe give me a hint.

The very next day, I got a call from the retreat organizer. Someone had canceled a booking unexpectedly, so there was now one spot available for the dates I wanted! "It's very strange," the organizer told me. "This never happens. I mean *never* happens. It is rare we ever get a cancelation but certainly never this close to the actual retreat."

"Well," I said, "I guess it was meant to be after all!"

After giving him my details and payment, I hung up the phone and thanked the universe profusely for fulfilling my request so quickly.

I packed the pictures of Ben, some of his sweatshirts to lounge in, and my other essentials, including a journal and pen, and hopped on a train to Devon.

September 9, 2009

Dear Ben,

> *Arrived yesterday evening at the detox retreat for a week of fasting, meditation, yoga, nutrition talks, life coaching, food intolerance testing, and . . . wait for it . . . two colonics a day! Yes, my body is going to get a good clear-out this week.*
>
> *The atmosphere is relaxed and the surroundings beautiful: small cottages in the middle of foliage and forests. The staff of four is friendly and helpful. I am told this is the thirtieth retreat they have done together.*
>
> *Tonight was my first experience trying bentonite clay. To my surprise, it was not as disgusting as I thought it would be. It is completely tasteless. Digestive enzymes, psyllium husks, and carrot juice (small amounts taken four times each day) are also on the menu. I've been drinking lots and lots of herbal tea. Thankfully, they have quite a good selection here, and I brought some of my own as well. Felt a little hungry when I arrived but really not too bad.*
>
> *I did have trouble getting to sleep last night. My mind was racing and my stomach churning, although, surprisingly, I did not want to eat. My stomach was grumbling loudly, but I wasn't hungry at all. That is a first! Remember how I used to get so angry when I hadn't eaten? Our code phrase was "food*

monster." When I used those two words, you knew I needed food and fast!

When I finally did drift off to sleep, I dreamed of you. Not sure where exactly in the country we were, but we were staying at a cottage somewhere. For some reason, I tried on your shirt. We both laughed at how big it was on me. It was so great to be laughing with you again.

Then the dream shifted, as dreams often do, and I was back at the retreat. Only you were still with me. It was a surprise seeing you there. I felt you probably wouldn't be very impressed with my chosen wardrobe of loungewear for the week, including a few of your sweatshirts.

Before you could comment, the dream shifted to colonics (which we are starting today). I will spare you the details on that one . . .

At the end of the week, I filled Ben in on the results.

Ben,

Well, it's been a week of ups and downs, a roller-coaster ride both physically and mentally. I have cried. I have heaved. I have laughed. I have slept . . . a lot. I rested a lot too. It's not easy to be active when you are fasting, although I did make it to yoga and tai chi almost every day.

I have found out I am not allergic to any foods. I have sweated in the sauna and nearly swam in the pool. Nearly. I have lost fourteen pounds (that's one stone in your language ;-).

My favorite part of the week was having a "La Stone Therapy" massage. The staff and guests who have had it were all raving about it, so I figured I should check it out. It was intensely relaxing, with hot stones and even some cold stones, which sounds unappealing but was actually quite a nice contrast.

When I arrived for my session, the therapist asked if I would prefer he talk or just be quiet so I could relax silently. I opted for the latter, as I normally find silent massages more relaxing and didn't want to be distracted with idle chitchat.

He acknowledged my choice, but as he continued the treatment, oddly enough he began talking anyway. Even more odd is the fact that I didn't stop him. He told me his background in health and wellness endeavors and how he had followed in the footsteps of his parents. There was mention at the orientation, when everyone was introducing themselves, that he and his long-time girlfriend were moving in together. Enjoying our conversation, I congratulated him on the move.

"Thanks," he replied. What he said next took me by surprise. "This is my first relationship since my wife died fourteen years ago. It hasn't been easy, but this move feels right."

I couldn't help but share with him my own situation and my reasons for being at the retreat. I told him about my need to detox on an emotional as well as a physical level before venturing on a new path.

We shared more of our personal stories, and he told me something I will remember forever. "It doesn't get easier. People who haven't been through it don't realize that. You don't get over it. You do get through it, though. And that person who is no longer physically with you continues to live in your heart for eternity. The sadness at their departure never leaves, but you move on, carrying the happy times you had with them in your heart."

His experiences spanned a longer time than mine, but I could relate. People had already started asking me if I was "over it" or insinuating that I should be by now, just over one year later. Some people around me are afraid to mention your name or look uncomfortable if I mention it. When I recount a story of us together, they quickly change the subject. I am sure some of them want desperately for me to be completely healed by now. They don't realize how deep the wound is of losing the love of your life. In the year that has passed, it seems like everyone around me is moving on with their lives while mine has stood still.

On my last day at the retreat, before we headed down to break our fast with our first meal in a week, I got an e-mail telling me the agency has found me a tenant for our home.

It is time for me to take my scarred heart and move on.

But don't worry, your spirit is coming with me.

All my love,
Aimee xoxoxoxoxo

Chapter 51

We can get away to a better place
If you let me take you there
We can go there now 'cause every second counts
Girl just let me take you there, take you there
—"Let Me Take You There," Plain White T's

England to Crete, April 2003

"Come on! Let's wake everyone up!"

After spending our first night of marital bliss together, Ben and I have an incredible amount of energy and wake up early. Although there was a lot of champagne popping at the reception, neither of us has a hangover. Once we are dressed and ready, we think it will be fun to wake the rest of the guests who have spent the night at Silchester House and get them down to breakfast so we can head out to our honeymoon.

We go door to door, knocking and cheering "Good morning!" and "Rise and shine!" Some guests are more conscious than others. A few are seriously suffering after partying until late. Ben and I run through the halls and giggle like schoolchildren before finally going downstairs and taking our places at the long breakfast table.

After breakfast, we gather our belongings and head out to the bright red Honda convertible Ben has been looking forward to taking for a ride. He puts down the top as the guests gather around to wish us farewell. Ben steps on the gas. I feel the wind flow through my hair, and we are off.

Hours later, we are at the airport waiting for our flight to Crete, where we have decided to honeymoon. Well, Ben decided, as he had some contacts there who got us a great deal. Crete is romantic while also being budget-friendly. Ben had wanted it to be a surprise, but I jokingly guessed it, and his mum, assuming I already knew, confirmed it. She was mortified that she had revealed the secret, but Ben and I were too amused by her reaction to be upset.

Our charter flight is delayed for hours. When we finally board, we take our economy seats in front of a little girl who insists on kicking the back of my seat. This continues although I shoot a look to her father. He does nothing to stop her, even after she begins to jump on her seat and scream loudly.

My blood pressure rises and I go from blissed out to pissed off relatively quickly. Married life should be easier than this, surely? What happened to traveling first class like we did to Paris?

Ben senses my thoughts even though I have kept silent, and apologizes that we have had to take a charter flight and not a private jet like he would have wanted. I assure him there is no problem.

No sooner do I finish the sentence than the little girl begins kicking the seat back again, only this time much harder. I let out a load groan and shoot daggers with my eyes at her father. The captain gets on the speaker to let us know we are still being delayed.

"*Ugh!*" I'm frustrated and want to be alone with my husband in our honeymoon suite.

Ben is beside himself, apologizing though I have not said a word of blame to him.

"It's okay, Ben. It's not your fault this sucks."

"I just wanted everything to be perfect."

"Well, things aren't perfect. Just deal with it. Nothing is perfect. It is what it is."

Tears well up in Ben's blue eyes. "But . . ." he says, "you said our wedding was perfect!"

He is right. I said it, and it is true. Our wedding was perfect. Just over twenty-four hours later, I'm upsetting him by caring about this minor bump in the road.

I take his hands in mine and look him straight in the eye. "This *is* perfect, Ben. We are married and I love you. This is going to be a fantastic honeymoon."

Ben calms down and beams a smile. We start giggling like kids again, and I rest my head on his shoulder. We no longer notice the girl kicking the seat. Soon the plane takes off and whisks us away on our honeymoon to happily-ever-after.

Chapter 52

You can go, you can start all over again
You can try to find a way to make another day go by
—"Someday," Rob Thomas

London, October 2009

I entered the new Terminal 5 at Heathrow Airport, soon to be whisked off to my new life. It had been a whirlwind past few days.

My leaving party was at one of our, well my, favorite French restaurants, Restaurant Noel. I had been frequenting it since Ben's death and always brought along my friends for special occasions, so I thought it was the perfect place. There was a good turnout, and I was delighted to see many of my friends, some of whom traveled quite a distance, even as far as from Manchester and Leeds, to wish me well on my new journey.

My good friends from Leeds, along with Alyson and Kevin, helped me move the last of my belongings out of the house. It suddenly seemed so empty, a shell of the place it had once been when Ben and I initially made it our home. How incredible the drastic changes in life were; nothing stayed the same.

I stood in the doorway for one last look. I could feel everyone's eyes on me, and I didn't want to linger. As I shut the door behind me, I felt everyone was waiting for me to cry. Instead, I chose to leave my tears in the house. I had been sobbing there for months. I took along the happy memories in my heart to keep forever.

We headed to a hotel in Richmond, West London, where I stayed for a day until leaving for, aptly, Richmond, Virginia.

When the black cab picked me up to take me to the airport, it was pouring rain. It pelted down loudly on the car and reminded me of all the tears I had shed in the last fifteen months. Rivers of tears. I hoped this new beginning brought with it more sunshine and less rain.

Text messages wishing me well in my new life kept coming during the cab ride and until I boarded the plane, where I finally had to shut off my cell phone.

As the plane took off, so began my new life.

Chapter 53

I finally stopped tripping on my youth
I finally got lost inside of you
I finally know that I needed to grow
And finally my mate has met my soul
— "Finally," Fergie

May 2003

Back from our honeymoon, and our married life at home begins. Our two weeks in Crete were amazing. We parasailed, visited historic ruins, soaked up the sun on beaches, and went for long drives in the mountains. We dined on delicious food and enjoyed lots of time in our honeymoon suite. Ben gifted me with the scrapbook he had been working on while we were apart, and I was touched he had taken the time and effort to give me a personal gift that spanned all the highlights of our relationship thus far.

We are still on a wedded high. We begin to make our way through the mountain of presents that have been magically transported from the wedding venue to our living room. Life as a married couple is good.

Chapter 54

As many times as I blink
I'll think of you tonight
I'll think of you tonight
—"Vanilla Twilight," Owl City

October 2009

L ife as a single woman was strange. In an effort to be helpful, friends and family suggested I should start making moves to "get out there" and start dating again. While I appreciated their concern, my head couldn't quite wrap around the idea just yet.

Instead, I lived the life of a singleton vicariously through the characters of *Sex and the City*. I watched the antics of Carrie, Miranda, Samantha, and Charlotte from the comfort of my couch while drinking wine and eating chocolate. Before leaving for the States, I had managed to get through the entire series. Six seasons. Twice.

My first stop in the States was with my brother and his family. Finally, I had the pleasure of meeting my niece, who had been born four months earlier. As my brother opened the front door, I got my first glimpse of Princess Pork Chop. (Although I know her name now, the title Princess Pork Chop has certainly stuck.)

She was the cutest baby I had ever seen, with huge blue eyes and a big, beaming smile. I was instantly in love.

This surprised me, as I'm not really a kid person. Nor am I a baby person. Sure, they were cute, but never had I felt a connection to one, and never the desire to have one of my own. Even growing up, when playing with dolls, I considered myself the babysitter or the ultra cool auntie.

While I still didn't want one of my own, I did feel a connection with this little girl I affectionately referred to as Princess Pork Chop. I was delighted to be her ultra cool auntie.

I was also grateful to spend so much time with her. Given she was only four months old, her days consisted of not a lot other than sleeping, eating, and lying around, but then again, that was pretty much all I was doing at the time too.

I had no idea what I wanted to do with my life, but I felt grateful to have moved home to the States. It created some necessary distance between me and the myriad of memories that tormented me at every turn in England. I had cut the cord from my old life and was now floating in the wind, unsure of where I would end up. For some reason, I was pretty calm. I knew everything was going to work out, even though I had no clue how that would come to be.

Princess Pork Chop, with her own recent experience of being cut from the cord, must have sensed my calmness. Whenever she was tired and fussy, I had a knack for soothing her. She would easily fall asleep, her little head resting on my shoulder.

One night, after I finally drifted off to sleep myself, I was with another blue-eyed beauty. Ben and I were together on a movie set. We were making the movie of our love story. Both of us were behind the cameras, directing the actors who were playing our parts. We finished for the day and headed home. The sun was shining again, and we entered a place unfamiliar to me in reality. I had some notion it was California, where we were shooting the movie. Brilliant light shone through the floor-to-ceiling windows that made up three walls of the large room. Our clothes and belongings were scattered about in organized chaos.

Ben picked up a suitcase and started packing some items in it. "I guess I should leave now," he said.

"What? Why? I don't want you to leave." My heart started beating faster as the fear of losing him grew in my chest.

"Well, I have to leave soon. The movie is nearly done."

"So?" I didn't understand.

Ben smiled as he continued to pack. When he looked up and saw my panic-stricken face, he stopped and came closer to me. "Aimee, the movie won't have the impact on people it is meant to have if I am still here. I have to go."

"Screw the movie," I said. "Stay." But Ben continued to pack.

I woke up crying. My heart was unable to cope with his departure, even if it happened in a dream and I knew he already left in reality long ago.

Though I wasn't surrounded by memories, I still thought of Ben every moment of every day. I guessed I always would. I was lonely and lost and praying to whatever higher power existed, whether God, Allah, Buddha, the universe, or some sacred energy, that I would be shown the way toward happiness again. I couldn't keep encroaching on other people's lives. I had to start living my own.

Chapter 55

Please don't change, please don't break
The only thing that seems to work at all is you
Please don't change at all from me
To you, and you to me
—"Real World," Matchbox Twenty

England 2003

"Where do you want to live? Really. Tell me the truth and we'll make it happen." Being married is easy, but I am finding living in England more difficult. Now that I am here "forever" rather than just one year, my perspective starts to change. I miss certain things that I never missed before. The transportation irritates me more than it did before. I am having some problems adjusting, but I don't know where I want to go or what I want to do. I answer Ben's question with a helpless look of self-pity.

"Okay. What do you miss here that you could have if we were living in the States?"

I think for a moment. What do I miss? I think harder before answering. The washing machine is whirring from our kitchen. "I miss having a dryer. And a big refrigerator."

Ben holds back a laugh and tries his best to keep a serious look on his face. "Okay. What else?"

"A separate room for the laundry rather than having it in the kitchen. And big roads. Big, straight roads that I feel comfortable driving on so I don't have to take the smelly, crowded train."

Ben struggles harder to keep his laughter inside, but it finally comes spewing out.

"What's so funny? You asked!"

"Do you realize you named off all things and no people?"

"Well, the person I miss the most is Dad, but neither of us wants to live in Detroit."

We both shiver at the thought. It's cold in Detroit.

"Besides," I say, "Dad would be busy all the time anyway, so even if we did live in the same state, we would probably not see him very often. He seems to have a busier social life than we do."

It is true. Dad really does live life to the fullest. He is quite the social butterfly from what I gather from our phone calls.

I continue, "The only person I really need to be close with is you."

Ben smiles.

"So I guess you want to stay in England because your family is here?" I sigh.

"Baby, I will go anywhere to be with you. If you want to move back to the States, then let's get going on it and make it happen. Yes, I love being near my family, but I would have fun in the States too. And they would visit us and we would visit them. The main thing is that we are both happy together. Tell me what will make you happy."

"*You* make me happy, Ben. It is silly I'm naming things rather than people. I'm sure I can adjust to our small fridge and air drying all my clothes again. I guess that now it just feels real that I'm not going back anytime soon. It makes me miss it more than before."

Ben comes over and hugs me. I make a mental note to start seeing the good in everything again.

The washing machine stops. Ben gets our clothes so we can put them on our air dryer. In the kitchen doorway, he looks over his shoulder.

"Oh, and baby," he says, "you don't really want straight roads. Where's the fun in that?"

Chapter 56

Everyday is a winding road
I get a little bit closer
Everyday is a faded sign
I get a little bit closer to feeling fine
—"Everyday is a Winding Road,"
Sheryl Crow

Virginia, November 2009

Life certainly had some exciting twists and turns.

I logged on to Facebook one morning and saw someone had commented on my status update, which read, "I love Virginia." The commenter was a woman, Tina, I recognized from culinary school. Although we had never spoken more than a few words, we connected as friends on Facebook. Her comment said she too was in Virginia. She asked me what part I was in. When I answered Richmond, she told me she was a few hours away, nearer the DC area in Fairfax. Tina asked if I was still raw vegan, and if so, how was I finding it? She went on to tell me she and her husband were finding it difficult to keep up with the healthy-eating lifestyle due to their busy schedules.

I asked when I should move in to be their personal chef. I was only half-joking. But I didn't expect her to respond.

As luck would have it, she did. "I know you are probably joking, but I would love for you to move in and be our personal chef for a while."

We discussed it more and traded phone numbers. Talking later, we agreed it was a great opportunity for both of us. We arranged to see each other the day after Thanksgiving. Perfect timing. I was so grateful.

Tina picked me up the day after Thanksgiving and took me back to her place. I didn't have a car and, at that moment, I didn't have a driver's license either. When I moved to New York, I rarely drove, and *rarely* turned to *never* when I moved to England. My license had expired long ago, and I had not driven a car in at least five years. I knew I would have to change that at some point, but the opportunity hadn't presented itself yet.

During the drive, Tina and I talked easily to each other. We shared stories and in some of mine I referred to "my husband." I still felt like the word *widow* was etched on my forehead and everyone knew. I realized that was not the case when Tina tentatively asked, "So, are you divorced?"

I pointed out the invisible etching on my forehead and she apologized. Briefly, I wondered how many apologies I had received in the last year and a half.

We continued our friendly chat and were both excited. I was delighted for the opportunity to get back in the kitchen, preparing raw vegan cuisine, and Tina was delighted to eat, enjoy, and feel better as a result.

The weeks passed by quickly. I had a lot of fun in the kitchen and spent hours every day preparing food and experimenting with new recipes. I learned a great deal, especially when we got stuck in the house for five days after a snowstorm and I was forced to go off-recipe and try new combinations.

The challenge sparked my interest to learn more about gourmet vegan cuisine. I discovered one of my favorite raw vegan chefs was opening a school to teach advanced techniques. Class would begin in March 2010, and that was perfect. In the meantime, I headed back to my brother's home to celebrate Christmas with him, his wife, and, of course, Princess Pork Chop, who was celebrating her very first Christmas. Just when I thought there could be nothing cuter than a baby in a Santa hat, New Year's Eve rolled around. Princess Pork Chop rang in the New Year with a purple-sequined headband, a big feather sticking out at the forehead and an even bigger grin on her face.

It was 2010, and I wondered what adventures the New Year would bring. First things first. I thought about how I should celebrate my birthday that month.

Chapter 57

I love you like a fat kid love cake
You know my style I say anything to make you smile
—"21 Questions," 50 Cent

London, January 2004

"Happy Birthday, baby! Okay, we need to go outside so you can open your gifts."

Ben picks up a rather large box covered in silver and white wrapping paper and motions me to the door.

"Why are we going outside? Why can't I open them here?"

"You'll see," he says with a glint in his eye. "C'mon, let's go!" He heads out the door. I hurriedly put on my sneakers, scarf, and jacket before following him. Outside, I pull on my gloves on this crisp and sunny winter day, intrigued.

He leads me to the park across the street from our apartment building. The huge smile never leaves his face, while the look of confusion grows on my own.

At a park bench, he presents me with the mysterious package.

"Hold on!" he says. He takes out his camera to snap a pic. I sit smiling, all the while wondering what on earth could possibly be in this box that I need to open outdoors.

"Okay, go ahead!"

No sooner does Ben give the go-ahead than my red gloves are ripping off the wrapping paper to discover what is inside. I see a piece of paper with the familiar logo of the London Underground on it. I look up at Ben, confused, before ripping open the box to find more silver-wrapped gifts inside.

"Okay, this one first." Ben points out a little package and holds his camera at the ready. I open it. It's a model of a Tube train. "Oh, thanks, honey. This is . . . great!" I smile graciously. Ben assures me that opening the next gift, contained in a silver gift bag, will clear up the puzzled look he sees on my face.

The bag is heavy. When I dip my hand in, I feel something familiar and it all makes sense. Before I can even pull out the hammer, Ben catches my reaction on camera. He knows how frustrated I have been around commuting. So he has given me a hammer to smash the model Tube train and get out some aggression. Now I see why we needed to be outside. I can't stop laughing. He is quite clever.

"Go on, then!" Ben urges me. "It's hammer time!" But I'm so touched by the gift and all the thought he put into it, I can't bring myself to smash it to pieces.

"Well, maybe there is something else you can hit to get out your aggression."

I look back in the box and see two remaining items. Opening them, I find boxing gloves in one and an inflatable punching bag in the other. "Now this I can hit!"

We rush back to the warmth of our apartment, change into our workout clothes, and go about inflating the punching bag. Once it's ready, we take turns, one of us punching the bag while the other takes pictures.

I congratulate Ben on his expert birthday celebration skills. From Paris to the park across the street, he never disappoints. Each birthday just keeps getting better.

Chapter 58

I thought that things like this get better with time
But I still need you, why is that?
You're the only image in my mind
So I still see you . . . around
—"I Miss You," Beyoncé

Boston, January 2010

I was on the train en route to Boston for my birthday. A friend I had met in London was now living there. I was thrilled she was up for celebrating with me and showing me around the city. It was an eleven-hour journey, and I was excited to have the time to rest, reflect, and read. By the time I got there, I was ready to party.

We had a great time catching up, exploring the city while we recounted various stories of our lives. The weather was mild, considering it was January, and we walked comfortably for miles. Our stops along the way included a few boutiques. We treated ourselves to manicures, pedicures, and new hairdos, and also indulged in some amazing food and drink. We dined at a raw vegan restaurant and ordered just about the entire menu, leaving no crumb, however small, behind.

Everything seemed to flow for the entire weekend, so smooth and effortless. We met up with another friend from culinary school and went to his vegan pizzeria. I'd never eaten vegan pizza that tasted so good.

Suddenly it was Monday, and time for me to head back to Virginia. As we walked to the train station, snow began coming down heavily. It was nice to be warm and cozy when I took my seat on the train for the long journey home.

Removing my journal from my bag a few hours after the train left the station, I wanted to share with Ben how I enjoyed my birthday. When I opened the book, memories of our life together came flooding back, washing all my new experiences of the weekend far away. I try to clutch them back, but other words flowed on paper like water from a broken dam.

Dear Ben,

It feels so lonely without you, but I'm pushing through. I miss my sunshine. I finally started writing the outline for "our story" in detail. It makes me miss you even more, if that is even possible. You made me feel whole. Now there is a big chunk of me missing.

I closed my eyes and saw Ben's beautiful smile and bright blue eyes. I could almost hear those words he so often used to say to me: "I love you . . . you are the one."

I drifted off to sleep, hoping to find him in my dreams.

Chapter 59

Baby you're the words and chapters
The sweetness in the morning after
You are the cry that turns to laughter
You're the hope that ends disaster
—"Warmer Climate," Snow Patrol

London, 2004

A beeping noise wakes me from my slumber. It's familiar, but in my half-awake state, I can't place it. The sound the garbage truck makes when backing up, perhaps? It feels too soon to be morning.

My gaze moves toward the window. Through the closed curtains, I see light. It looks different from natural sunlight: brighter, more orange. The sound gets louder, more screeching. Dragging myself out of bed, I move to the window, pull back the curtains, and let out a blood-curdling scream.

Flames are the source of the bright light breaking through pitch darkness. Lots of flames. Coming from cars in the parking lot. My eyesight is lacking without my contacts, but I see figures of men surrounding the flames, screaming. Are they in the midst of setting more on fire?

Ben wakes up in bed behind me and sleepily approaches the window, where his eyes meet with the scene in the parking lot. He is normally a deep sleeper but comes to attention immediately, turns on the light, and starts getting dressed without saying a word.

"Wait! Where are you going? There are cars on fire down there!"

"I know! Mine is one of them!"

"Oh." I couldn't make that out with my eyesight. I look outside again and see the men are still jumping around the flames. "But you can't go out there, honey! It's dangerous!" What did Ben plan to do? Confront the bunch of hooligans who had set his car ablaze?

He shoots me a look of confusion before running out the door. I shout after him, "You're my hero!"

Then I run to the bathroom to get my glasses and return to the window. With clear eyesight, I see the men are not hooligans at all, but firemen trying to put out the flames. Their big fire truck is the source of the noise that originally woke me up. I feel a little silly, as I now understand why Ben looked so perplexed at my mention of danger.

Hours later, with the fire cleared and me seeing clearly thanks to my contacts, Ben and I sit in the living room. He makes a phone call. The flames engulfed only one half of his car. It caught fire from the car parked next to it that had been stolen earlier in the evening. We had gone down earlier to see it, and were amazed that if you just looked from one side, the car looked absolutely fine. The other side was completely burned through; only a skeleton remained.

The company Ben works for has leased the car to him, and he is calling to request a new car.

He hangs up the phone. "That was easy. I'll have a new car by this evening. I just need to get a ride to work."

"We are very lucky," I add. "That could have been a lot worse. We didn't lose anything."

"Well," Ben counters, "I can't seem to get the Eminem CD to come out of the CD player. I gave up trying. It's gone."

I can't help but giggle.

"Okay, I know; it's just a CD. We are very lucky. And who would have thought it would be so easy to get another car? All it took was a phone call."

I agree.

"And it makes for a great story to tell people. What was that you said again when I ran out the door?"

"Ha ha. You are still my hero, even if there was little danger in going downstairs."

Ben laughs before kissing me and heading out the door. He has a proud smile on his face, pleased with himself for racking up another embarrassing story about me.

Chapter 60

And you cast your fears aside
And you know you can survive
So when you feel like hope is gone
Look inside you and be strong
And you'll finally see the truth
That a hero lies in you
—"Hero," Mariah Carey

Oklahoma City, March 2010

The taxi wove its way through the streets lined and lit up with strip malls and fast food joints. It pulled up at the entrance of my hotel. I checked in at the front desk and made my way to my room. As I closed the door behind me, it hit me.

I had no idea what I was doing.

Coming to Oklahoma City for culinary school had seemed like a great idea, an excellent opportunity to sharpen my skills, make new friends, and plan out my next move. Perfect.

Now I was there.

In Oklahoma City, a city I had never visited before.

Where I knew no one.

To make matters more awkward, I hadn't gotten around to getting my driver's license yet, much less a car. Oklahoma City was not much of a walking city. I guessed I should have researched that more.

I had no idea how I was even going to get to class on the first day.

Slumping back on the bed with my hands over my face, I wondered what Ben would think of me now.

Chapter 61

I am the sound of love's arriving
Echoed softly on the sand
Lay your head upon my shoulder
Lay your hand within my hand
I give you all that I am
—"All That I Am," Rob Thomas

England to Australia, 2004

"I think that is fantastic news!" I hear Ben say on the phone. "Congratulations!"

He hangs up the phone to share with me that our friends, who met at our wedding last year, are getting married. The wedding is in Australia. Perfect timing for that honeymoon we had originally planned.

The day to depart England finally comes and we are on our first twenty-four-hour flight, landing in Melbourne. Our plan is to stay there for a few days before heading to Sydney, and then to meet up with our friends at the wedding on the Whitsunday coast.

It's three weeks of magic. We get up close to koalas, kangaroos, and wombats, as well some penguins on Philip Island. We drive the Great Ocean Road and drink our way through the wineries in the Yarra Valley. We go to the Sydney Opera House and climb Sydney Bridge. We move on to sunbathe on Bondi Beach before heading to the Whitsunday coast, where we snorkel at the Great Barrier Reef and enjoy long walks on beaches with white sand and clear waters. We spend time in our suite overlooking the ocean, complete with a hot tub and hammock for two on the balcony. We witness one of the most beautiful weddings ever.

One might think we would be disappointed to come back from our adventures. Strangely, the opposite is true. As we board our twenty-four-hour flight to London, there are genuine smiles on our faces. We now both feel happy to call England home.

Chapter 62

You are there when I'm a mess
You talked me down from every ledge
You give me strength, boy you're the best
And you're the only one who's ever passed every test
—"Ain't No Other Man," Christina Aguilera

Oklahoma City, May 2010

Dear Ben,

    I found a temporary home in OKC. Turns out all that worrying was unnecessary, as everything worked out. My classmates have been amazing and I'm sharing an apartment with one of my fellow chefs-in-training, which has been a lot of fun.

    It's been an emotional ride with lots of up and downs. Yesterday was my second academy dinner project, for which we are required create, prepare, and serve up a three-course meal for diners at the restaurant. This time around we had the added benefit of having our classmates as part of our teams, rather than doing it all on our own.

    The menu I created consisted of crab cakes with rémoulade and corn salsa, gumbo, and bananas Foster for dessert. I know you were not really excited about raw vegan cuisine, but I think you would have liked this—certainly the dessert. Either way, I know you would have been excited for me. I wish you were here.

When I woke up on the day my menu was to be presented, I felt really low. No one else was excited by my accomplishment. Why should I be? Did it even matter? Trying to put on my happiest face and best attitude, I opened my laptop to go online. We had not been getting good reception recently, so I was impressed when getting online was easy.

Then I saw it. An article saying a famous young actress's husband died, five months after her own sudden death. The article talked about how they were self-confessed soul mates and stated the cause of his death was unknown.

Five months apart. I was jealous. It took me back to the day I started packing up your things, which was five months after you died. I sat there wondering why I hadn't died yet. We were self-confessed soul mates too. Why was I still here, years later? It didn't seem fair. No one cared I was here. Why couldn't I just be with you again?

I was angry, and I took my anger to school with me. It caused conflict. I knew I had to let it go, so I did. But I fully intended to pick up my anger again after my food was sold and I could go home.

The menu was a great success. I sold out quickly and received many compliments from happy diners. As I was cleaning up, smiling at my victory, I heard it. It's something I had never heard before at the restaurant. Christina Aguilera's voice began blaring out of the speakers, singing "Ain't No Other Man."

The song I used to sing to you. The song that was played as they carried your red coffin down the aisle for your final celebration.

It was at that moment that I could feel you celebrating with me.

Thank you for being there. You are with me always.

Love,
Aimee

Chapter 63

When you feel helpless, when you are low
I'll be the light upon the path to guide you home
I'll fill the spaces in your heart, I will remind you who you are
And when you shine just like a star, I'll let you go
—"I'll Be Waiting," Bliss

London, 2004

"Well, as long as we are together, I wouldn't mind."

Ben shoots me a stern look. "Aimee. Be realistic."

Our goal is to find and buy a house within our budget. Ben suggests Hounslow, where we can have a garden and outdoor space. My preference is Richmond, a more expensive part of London. Ben acknowledges Richmond is an option if we are prepared to live in smaller quarters, which he refers to as "a box." Apparently, this is not realistic.

"Well . . ." I begin. But with no real defense, I counteract his stern look with one of sadness tinged with hope, tears welling in my eyes.

"Aimee! Really. Don't look at me like that. You know what I am saying is true, and you *know* you do not want to live in a smaller space than we have now. Where would we put all your shoes?" he adds with a grin.

"What about all *your* shoes?" For a guy, Ben owns a *lot* of shoes. Nearly as many as I did, and most of them sneakers in crazy colors.

"Well, precisely. That's why we are getting a house in Hounslow."

"Oh." I decide to go back to my original plan. I gaze at him forlornly, my eyes watering once again.

"Aimee, really," he responds, avoiding my gaze. "Let's just look at a few houses in the area, and then we'll make the decision about where we want to live."

I think about it for a minute.

"Okay," I agree.

There is no harm in looking.

Chapter 64

I can't let you go
Can't let you go
You're part of my soul
You're all that I know
—"Can't Let You Go," Matchbox 20

NYC, July 16, 2010

Ben,

Hi there. It's been a while since I've written . . . sorry about that. I think of you every moment of every day and feel your presence with me all the time, but don't always pick up a pen and transfer my thoughts to you on paper. Thought it might be nice to change that today and let you know how I'm doing and what I've been up to . . .

At this moment, I'm looking at Cowgirl Hall of Fame as I sit across the street at Starbucks, sipping on a latte. Cowgirl is the place where our love story began and where we shared our very first kiss. I know you know that . . . but just in case you forgot.

I'm in NYC for about a month, oddly enough staying with a friend who lives around the corner from Cowgirl Hall of

Fame. It surprised me to see it there suddenly, and the memories instantly flooded back. I couldn't bring myself to go in, but I peeked through the window earlier while pretending to look at the menu.

Two years later and I still can't believe you are gone. It's silly, I know. Perhaps you have forgotten all about me, but you are engraved deeply in my heart for eternity.

It's strange you left this world on the sixteenth. The sixteenth was the day you proposed to me. In honor of your life, my friend and I are celebrating this day. After all, you were the one who taught me how to live life, and I feel even more compelled on this day to show you I've learned the lesson well. We are celebrating at an Egyptian restaurant tonight. But before we head off to indulge in delicious food and drink, we'll be getting our nails done and doing some shopping. I've had my eye on some deep purple shoes of which I'm sure you would approve.

I'm planning my next move while I'm here. There are some potential clients in various states, and I just may have snagged an internship in Hawaii! Remember how we were going to go there and renew our vows for our ten-year wedding anniversary? Anyway, we shall see. I'm back to Virginia soon to attend Princess Pork Chop's first birthday party. Time certainly does fly.

Anyway, I have no idea where I'll call "home" next, but I am kind of excited to see how this plays out. I'll keep you posted.

Thanks for sharing your time here with me. I love you forever.

Aimee xoxoxoxoxxoxo

Chapter 65

Do you know where you're going to?
Do you like the things that life is showing you?
Where are you going to?
Do you know?
—"Do You Know Where You're Going To?"
Mariah Carey

London, 2004

"**I**t's our home," I declare as soon as we leave the house.

"Well," Ben says, not wanting to be too enthusiastic in front of the estate agent, "it was rather nice, but we need to think about it."

Once we are out of the agent's earshot, our conversation continues.

"It's a little out of our price range, Aimee."

"Ben. It's our home. I see us living there. When I see it, it happens."

"Yes, but . . ."

"There is no 'but'! If you want to live in Hounslow, we will live in *this* house."

We have been searching for a home in the area with no luck. Tonight, we reluctantly went to see another one after work, and it is exactly what we were looking for. It is perfect.

"It's ten thousand above our budget."

"I'm not letting a little money get in the way of us living in our dream home."

"Baby. I totally understand. I love the house too. It does suit our needs and is the nicest house we have seen by far. However, the money is . . ."

"Something we will find if she is not willing to lower the price."

The estate agent is close enough to hear our last sentences and interrupts. "She might be willing to drop the price. Would you like to put in an offer?"

"Yes!" I answer before Ben can stop me. He stares at me in surprise, his mouth half-open, speechless, as we get back in our car.

"You want the house, don't you?" I ask.

"I do." He nods.

"Well then, let's get it. Don't worry; it's all going to work out."

I don't know exactly how, but I know this to be true.

Chapter 66

And I move all directions
To the corners and the outskirts
While the lovers and the lonely
Start to whisper all about me
And if I stand here silent
I almost start to feel you fading in
Telling me hold on
Cuz it's gonna be alright
—"When The Heartache Ends,"
Rob Thomas

Richmond, August 2010

Everything is going to work out. Only good lies before me.

That was the mantra I kept telling myself when things kept falling through. When I arrived in Richmond for Princess Pork Chop's very first birthday party, it looked like the internship in Hawaii was a sure thing. But once I arrived, I sent message after message to get the details I needed to make arrangements. Days turned into weeks and still no answer.

To explore my options, I followed up with potential clients in Oklahoma City, DC, and Los Angeles. Every one of them fell through over the weeks. I wondered what was going on. More importantly, I wondered where I was going to go.

My brother caught me looking at apartments in Richmond one day and offered to go see some places with me. I was sure Hawaii would get back to me any day now, but there was no harm in looking.

Another week passed and still no word from Hawaii. Meanwhile, we found a place that seemed perfect if I did decide to stay in the area. It was the right price and in a great location.

I checked my e-mail one final time before signing a year's lease. It was done. I was staying in Richmond for at least a year.

The next day I opened my e-mail and saw what I had been waiting for all that time: an invitation to Hawaii with all the details included, along with an apology for not responding sooner. I let out a sigh before responding that I now had to decline the internship.

Well, Richmond, I thought. *You had better have something pretty fantastic in store for me here.*

Chapter 67

We may never find our reason to shine
But here and now this is our time
And I may never find the meaning of life
But for this moment I am fine
—"Streetcorner Symphony," Rob Thomas

London, April 2004

I t all works out. We get the house and are moving in. Now we just need to buy furniture, as the apartment we are currently living in came furnished.

We begin shopping together, and I'm amazed by how easy it is. Ben and I agree on decor: clean, modern, and uncluttered. We agree on the same bed frame and futon, and spend more on our living room set than we intended but agree it's worth it. Every piece that enters our home we carefully pick out together. It makes the house seem that much more special. We have a home. Our home.

Chapter 68

I wake in the morning tired of sleeping
Get in the shower and make my bed alone
I put on my makeup talking to the mirror
Ready for a new day without you
—"My Hands," Leona Lewis

Richmond, August 2010

I looked around my new home. A new bookshelf stood proudly in the living room. That was about all that was standing there. I had yet to buy any more furniture. I wasn't entirely committed to staying in Richmond, so I didn't want to purchase anything unnecessary that might hold me back from leaving later. Like a couch . . .

The essentials were covered: my kitchen was well stocked, my closet was full of shoes and clothes, and there was plenty to read. The air mattress that had followed me from Oklahoma City to New York City was inflated in my bedroom. It was bliss.

There was something oddly satisfying about owning little in the way of things. It was soul-cleansing. It was a fresh start for the many new adventures ahead of me. I grabbed a book and headed to my bedroom, once again the queen of my own domain.

I came to the realization that at that point, there was only me. Only me to worry about. Somehow, there was freedom in knowing that.

Chapter 69

Why is it the ones you love
That make it all so hard on you
Then you let it fall behind
And in the back of your mind
You feel my loving shine
You think you might be saved
—"Fallin' To Pieces," Rob Thomas

London to Detroit, October 2004

"What's wrong?"

I'm on the phone with my dad, who is more quiet than normal.

"Well, I should tell you something. It's no big deal, but I know you would be mad if I didn't tell you."

"Okay. What is it?"

"It's nothing. I was having some problems. I went to the doctor and, well, it turns out they found something and . . . Well, it's no big deal, but . . . I'm getting my prostate out."

"What? Why? It's not cancer, right?" My mom had been diagnosed with breast cancer a few months ago. Surely, it isn't possible for both parents to get cancer in the same year. That seems really unfair. I hope there is some other explanation as to why Dad suddenly needs his prostate removed.

His silence on the other end of the line is not reassuring.

"Dad!"

"They caught it early, Aimee, so really, there is no reason to worry. This is a standard procedure. I'm going to be fine. I just thought you should know."

"Of course I should know! When is the surgery? I'll book my flight."

"It's not necessary, really. I'll be fine."

"Dad. I'm booking my flight."

I feel terrible for living in England, which suddenly feels so far away. Dad tells me when he is scheduled to go in for surgery, and I book the next flight to Detroit. Although Ben wants to accompany me, our finances are limited, given the recent purchase of the house and furniture. Just one last-minute flight proves to be out of budget.

Ben takes me to the airport and tells me, "Tell your dad this being sick business is not tolerated. He needs to get better and fast!" Ben smiles at me while acting as if he's laying down the law. "Seriously, Aimee, send him my best. I hope it's not serious and he gets better soon."

Dad is in good spirits and seems his normal self, greeting me with a big grin and giving me a bear hug to welcome my arrival.

My brother has come to town as well. It is strange Ben is not here. When we are not at the doctor's office, we go out to eat and shop as a family. Dad mentions on more than one occasion, "You know who would like it here? Ben." Each time he smiles and then recounts the tale of shopping for winter hats with Ben. Each time, we all laugh. Ben is definitely part of the family.

As the week goes on, Dad's surgery is pushed back, my mom suffers badly from the effects of chemo, and my grandmother has a heart attack. I feel like I have stepped into the Twilight Zone. I wish Ben could be there with us. It's the anniversary of our first date, and Ben has packed a card in my suitcase for me to find once I arrive. I'm grateful for e-mail.

Hi hon,

Thanks so much for the card. I really miss being with you, especially on our anniversary! Will make it up to you when I get back.

Looks like Dad's surgery will be next Monday, although we will know more tomorrow. I'm going to give the company a ring in the morning and extend my leave another few days. I'll let you know the details once I change my flight.

Nan's surgery was successful and doctors are optimistic she will make a full recovery. We are going to the hospital today to see her, so it is unlikely I will be home when you call. I am off tomorrow to see my mom, will let her know you said "hello"!

Anyway, I hope you are okay. I really miss you. You are real, right? Seems like I've stepped into someone else's life and you were just a dream. I keep checking my sparkly ring to remind myself you are still out there. I love you.

Oh! I almost forgot! We went to shopping yesterday and I got you some cool *stuff! No Pistons jersey, I'm afraid. I know you requested one but when we looked at them everyone agreed that it was not really your style . . .*

Feels like it has been years since I have spoken to you. Hope you are having fun without me.

Love you,
Aimee
XOXOOXOX

Hello baby,

I am going to miss you so much for another week, but I understand and you need to be there.

Good news on your Nan, send my love!

I respect your judgment on the Pistons jersey and am excited by the other stuff you have bought!

Really, though, I just need you. I am feeling very lost without you.

I am out here and real!

Send everybody my love!

Love you loads!

Ben

XOXO

Hello beautiful,

I did go running after calling you. I misjudged the way the clouds were going and got very wet! Doh!

Forgot to wish your dad all the luck in the world for the op on Monday. If I don't speak to you before, give him a hug for me!

Love you!

Ben

The operation is successful and Dad is recuperating. It's strange and unsettling to see him unwell. As far back as I can remember, Dad has never had a bad cold, much less a life-threatening illness. He assures me he is fine. With a heavy heart and hopeful attitude, I head back home to my husband. I'm so happy and grateful to be married to the best husband in the world.

Chapter 70

Just keep trying and trying
It's just a matter of timing
Though the grinding is tiring
Don't let it stop you from smiling
—"Lil Star," Kelis

Richmond, September 2010

Trying to put a happy face on being single again was not easy. I regretted all the well-intentioned advice I used to give my single friends. It had all come back to bite me in the butt. In an attempt to shut them up, I finally put my profile on an online dating service.

The only one not happy about this was my mom. She thought it was dangerous. I assured her I was cautious and confessed my real feelings.

"Look, Mom. This is simply a way to meet people in a new place. I'm not looking for the next love of my life. It's dipping a toe back in the dating scene and perhaps making some new friends."

"Well, I certainly hope you have another love in your life. You deserve it, and I don't want you to be alone."

"When I meet the next love of my life, it won't be on a dating site. Don't ask me how, but I know this to be true. Dating sites are great, and I know they bring people together, but as far as a love match, I just know I'll meet him somewhere else."

"You know what? I think you're right." For once, Mom agreed with me.

I appreciated that Mom worried. I had not felt worry in a while. I just felt numb.

Chapter 71

Can't explain all the feelings that you're making me feel
My heart's in overdrive and you're behind the steering wheel
—"I Believe in a Thing Called Love," Lemar

England, September 2004

Fear is rising in my throat as I watch the plane dive down . . . down . . . and down . . . I hold my breath and wonder if I have made the biggest mistake of my life.

For Ben's birthday last month, I wanted to gift him with something adventurous. After a lot of thought, consideration, and online research, I settle on a glider flight. Ben will be in the small plane with a licensed pilot. Once up in the air, he will get to take the controls at some point. It is right up Ben's alley; he loves this kind of stuff.

When I proudly tell a bunch of my friends of the gift, they are apprehensive and ask if I am worried at all for his safety. I assure them it is indeed safe and the company reputable. Besides, I have never heard or read of anyone getting injured on these flights.

That is, until the day before Ben is scheduled to fly. I open the paper and see an article detailing an accidental death on a glider flight. Shit.

Ben is excited, and I can't possibly cancel just because I'm suddenly afraid. I pray to the powers that be for his safety.

Now I sit wondering if my prayers have gone unanswered as the glider nosedives toward the ground.

Just when I'm about to burst into tears, vomit, faint, or all of the above, the plane does a loop.

My breath comes back and my heart starts to beat again.

Ben gets out of the glider, exhilarated. He whispers in my ear that he is also slightly nauseous. I too feel nauseous; watching his flight has been quite an emotional rollercoaster. His family is there and watched along with me. When they suggest lunch, we both wince at the thought of food.

On our way home, Ben confesses, "I loved the gift and it was great fun, but I think once was enough. I don't feel the need to do that again."

Chapter 72

'Cause maybe someday we'll figure all this out
We'll put an end to all our doubt
Try to find a way to just feel better now that
Maybe someday we'll live our lives out loud
We'll be better off somehow, someday
—"Someday," Rob Thomas

Richmond, November 2010

I really didn't want to do this again. While shopping for furniture and housewares might be fun for some people, for me it was not. I would much rather have focused my time and energy elsewhere.

Hence, my one-bedroom apartment remained sparse. I finally purchased a real bed and moved my trusty old air mattress to the living room to act as a couch. A desk was my second purchase, giving me a place to do work other than on the floor or at the local Starbucks.

I was making friends quickly, one being a feng shui consultant. While I taught her how to juice and enjoy a healthier diet, she showed me how to make my house more "homey." She helped me pick out some bedroom curtains and accent items. She moved things around in my kitchen to make it more user-friendly and appear a little bigger. We hung up the curtains together, and I was amazed how such a little thing made such a huge difference.

After I thanked her for all her help, my friend headed out into the torrential rain. Finally, it seemed like things were starting to feel like home. Was my life finally looking up? I'd been making the best out of less than ideal situations for what felt like forever. Maybe things were starting to change and become easier.

I went back into the bedroom to admire my new curtains once again. As I stood staring at them, I noticed a stain on one. How strange I hadn't seen it before, I thought. As I continued to look at it, it got bigger and bigger. Confused, I walked over to see if my eyes were playing tricks on me.

When I pulled the curtain back, I realized the torrential rain had made it inside my room. Water poured down the closed windows and the walls and pooled into the carpet.

No. I sigh. Turns out life was not getting easier.

Chapter 73

Oh I'll stay with you through the ups and the downs
Oh I'll stay with you when no one else is around
And when the dark clouds arrive
I will stay by your side
I know we'll be alright
I will stay with you
—"Stay With You," John Legend

Great Britain, 2006

"You said this was going to be *easy*! You lied!"

"Well, if I had told you the truth, you never would have agreed to do it."

Ben is right. Now I have agreed to do it, and there is no backing out.

We are signed up for the Three Peak Challenge. The challenge consists of climbing the three highest peaks in the United Kingdom within twenty-four hours. The start point is at Ben Nevis, the highest peak in Scotland. Then you drive to Scafell Pike in England, and end by walking up the last peak, Snowden, in Wales.

We are currently at Snowden on our first training hike. Ben has depicted Snowden as "incredibly easy" and says there is a paved walking trail all the way up to the summit. The first assertion is questionable, the second an outright lie, and I wonder how I ever believed any of it in the first place.

"Wait!" I say, coming to a realization while hurdling another rock formation. "Were you lying about this being the easiest one of the three?"

"Oh no, that part is true! The others I reckon will be harder than this."

I stop and stand with my mouth hanging open. This is going to be interesting. We are in a team with two of Ben's work colleagues, both male. I don't want to be the girl lagging behind and bringing down the team. I mentally commit myself right then to do a ton of training.

Ben reads my thoughts. "This is the first of many training days. Don't worry; it will get easier."

I wonder if that is another one of his fibs. But when we finally make it to the top of Snowden, we stand together witnessing a breathtaking view. We have made it. If we can do this, what else can we do?

Over the weeks ahead, we stick to our training schedule, most often going to Box Hill on the weekends, walking up and down for hours and getting our bodies used to steep inclines. We purchase walking sticks, which are surprisingly useful, especially at taking the pressure off your knees when walking downhill.

Before we know it, the event is upon us. Our team of five (four climbers plus one driver), along with all our equipment and food supplies, arrives in Scotland. We have dinner after checking in to the B and B and then call it an early night. We are scheduled for a five o'clock start. We will need all our energy as it will be a full twenty-four hours, or close to it, until we finish.

The day starts out cold and dark. The scream of the alarm clock comes too soon. While I'm putting on my layers of thermals, Ben thanks me for taking part in this with him.

"I know it wasn't really your thing when we started. But you are doing really well, and it's been fun training with you. I'm glad we are doing this together." He smiles before giving me a kiss.

It has been fun. Never had I thought I could do this before. Ben has inspired me to new heights . . . quite literally.

We head out to tackle Ben Nevis. As we walk up the mountain, the darkness gives way to light. By the time we reach the peak, the view is clear and sunny. This apparently is very rare; we are told there are a limited number of clear days at the peak, a handful at most during any given year. It makes the moment of enjoying the view all the more sweet.

But we cannot enjoy it for too long, as there are still two more peaks to climb. Heading down seems to take much longer than going up. And is much more difficult, even with the added benefit of the walking sticks. Just when I think that we will surely reach the depths of hell if we keep going down, or at least the core of the earth, we reach ground level and the finish line. I head straight to the ladies' room and meet the boys back at the van to begin our journey to Scafell Pike.

Ben and I are in the front bench of the van while our two hiking teammates take up the back one. The coolers are stored in the front. Ben and I open them and start dishing out the abundant food supplies.

In the back, the men are having a contest over whose socks smell the worst. I look at Ben.

"Do you want to smell my socks?" I ask in earnest.

Ben contorts his face at the thought. "No! Why on earth would I want to do that, Aimee? Yuck!"

"I just wanted to fit in with the group," I say in a soft voice, and go back to eating my pasta in a plastic bowl.

First famished, now sleepy, I close my eyes as we hit some traffic on the roadway. When I open them two hours later, we have moved less than two miles. The traffic keeps us longer than we would like, but we finally make it to Scafell Pike.

It's much more gravelly than Ben Nevis, and I nearly lose my footing a few times, but I'm proud to be keeping up with the boys. All that training has certainly paid off. Each of us reaches a low point during the climb except for Ben. It is not the first time that I wonder if he has superhuman powers. He smiles, laughs, jokes, and encourages all of us to the top, which we finally reach before sunset. We hold up a large company sign while taking a photo to prove we made it to the top.

Again, getting down is harder, but this time due to the quickly fading light and gravelly undertow. We all make it safely, and we are back in the car for more food and sleep before Snowden.

Once on the mountain, our headlamps shine through the fog and darkness. Either I slept too much or too little on the journey here, because I feel like I'm walking in a dream. I must look like it too, as Ben stops me a few times to ask if I am okay. He holds my hand and helps me whenever possible.

The winds pick up and it's wet, making it easy to slip. Each of has a near fall. Each of us except Ben, who trudges forward confidently.

By the time we make it to the summit, there are sixty-mile-an-hour winds, rain, and fog. As we start our journey down, the peak is closed as it becomes too dangerous.

The finish line is finally in sight. In sight, but still far away. Ben begins to pick up pace, but my legs won't go any faster. Near the end, he begins to sprint. Watching him from behind, I know I will get there—just not as quick as Ben.

Chapter 74

But I'll miss your arms around me
I'd send a postcard to you, dear
'Cause I wish you were here
—"Vanilla Twilight," Owl City

February 14, 2011

Dear Ben,

Are you ready for me yet? Every day, I'm striving to do my best, so I can be with you again.

It's Valentine's Day. On our first Valentine's Day together, you gifted me with a scrapbook you had made of our relationship up to that point, including our first "date" of rock climbing, although we went as friends. The next year we celebrated at a fancy restaurant in London amid heart confetti and rose petals. We sat close to each other on a comfy bench and enjoyed our three-course meal, courtesy of a raffle prize I had recently won.

You have been gone nearly three years yet still provided me with a gift today.

To kick-start my business here, I began selling homemade chocolate truffles, brownies, and cookies for the Valentine's Day *holiday. It actually went quite well and I was proud of my accomplishment. But I guess you already knew that.*

All my orders done and sent, I was home alone with no plans to go out. There was a large box of paperwork my brother returned to me a few weeks ago. He had been storing it since I first moved to London. For weeks, I had been telling myself I should go through the paperwork but just kept putting it off. Until today.

Finally, I pulled the plastic folders out of the box and started going through them. I found old invoices, bank statements, paycheck stubs, receipts . . . and then I came across a bit of sunshine. Among the dull monotony of white paper was a bright yellow envelope. Inside was a brightly colored card with the Disney character Tigger and the words "I'm so happy for you" on the front. Inside, the card read, "I'll be bouncing all day! Congratulations!"

It was not signed or marked inside. I had a thought that maybe I had bought this for you and, for some reason, neglected to give it to you. Then I turned the card over and saw your familiar handwriting. It read, "To Aimee, How could I resist such a card?! You know I will be thinking of you and bouncing of course! Lots of love, Ben XOXO PS: Wish I could be there."

When I read the last line, I began to cry. I wish you were here too. And yes, you would have liked my Valentine's Day treats.

It took me a while to remember, but you gave me the card on the day I graduated from college in 2001. The words you wrote over ten years ago were just as appropriate for today.

I felt so loved. It made me wonder if I had made you feel as loved. As I continued through the paperwork, I got my answer. This one was in a blue envelope adorned with a heart and arrow on the back and addressed to "Miss DuFresne." It was your first birthday card to me, and read, "Aimee, Aimee, Aimee . . . .

Since we have started seeing each other, my world has taken a totally unexpected turn. Yet you make me feel so happy, and I constantly think of you. When I am with you, I enter a dreamy state in which the rest of the world does not exist. You even make me come out of my emotional shell—quite a feat! I love you, Ben xxx"

Am I crazy? Do I want to be with you so badly that I am reading too much into minor details and memories?

Do you even miss me?

I miss you.

Happy Valentine's Day, my love.

Aimee

I went to sleep that night wondering. Maybe I was going crazy and Ben didn't even miss me at all. How would I know?

The next day, I started doing some work and writing notes in an old notebook I had recently found. The notebook must have been older than I thought . . . As I scribbled a list of topics to write about, I noticed something was written on the next page. I flipped the sheet to see written in big, bold letters, "MISSING YOU ALREADY! LOVE YOU! Ben xxx"

I had my answer. Thanks, Ben.

Chapter 75

White. A blank page or canvas. His favorite. So many possibilities.
—Sunday in the Park with George

London, 2006

"Thanks, baby! This is the perfect solution to our problem!"

Ben has just opened my gift of three small, white canvases and paints in red, black, and silver. A few months earlier, we had taken a trip to Wales and discovered an artist whose work we absolutely loved. We bought a small piece of her work for our bedroom and commissioned her to do a painting for our new home. When it arrives, Ben and I agree it is perfect. A large, abstract painting of geometric shapes and swirls in red, black, and silver takes pride of place in our living room.

We both love and admire the painting very much. We are interested in adding some smaller paintings to accent it. After several attempts to get in touch with the artist, it seems she has disappeared. Ben has joked on a few occasions that we could probably make the paintings ourselves.

So I decide to buy the materials and put our artistic skills to the test.

To be honest, my faith lies entirely with Ben. My own artistic skills are lacking, to say the least. Ben doesn't let me down or let me off the hook. While he recreates the original painting's geometric shapes in shades of black and red, I am given the task of creating the perfect silver swirls. Just as I'm squeezing silver paint on the final spiral, an air bubble splatters, casting silver spots all over Ben's masterpiece.

I'm convinced it's ruined. But, with a few expert brushstrokes, Ben makes it all better.

Chapter 76

I talk about you now and go a day without crying
I go out with my friends now, I stay home all alone
And I don't see you everywhere and I can say your name easily
I laugh a bit louder without you
And I see different shades now and I'm almost never afraid now
But when I think I'll be okay I am always wrong
    —"My Hands," Leona Lewis

Richmond, July 14, 2011

Ben,

> *I keep hoping things will get better and I'll begin to fit into this new life without you. Like a shirt that is too tight, I keep pulling, squeezing, and maneuvering myself to make it work. Just when I think I've been successful, the seams burst and a huge hole opens. The hole where my heart used to be, where you used to be.*

> *Things have been going well, the hole well hidden as I covered it over with a thin blanket of new friends and fun times. But last night I fell through and kept falling into the depths of darkness. I arrived home from a friend's house and began to cry. I cried my eyes out, mascara streaming down my face in rivers. I miss you. I miss being loved. I miss feeling loved and loving you so freely.*

I miss how we used to talk about anything and everything, and how it was so easy and comfortable to be with you. I miss how excited we both were about life and our ambitions.

What remains of your physical being is stored in a box in my closet. I couldn't bear to leave England without you. Your mum was storing your ashes, and she decorated the plain brown box with colorful photos of you taken throughout your life. There is a picture of baby Ben clutching the stuffed Tigger his Nan had sewn for him, and a picture of us on our wedding day surrounded by family and friends. On the top of the box is a large photo of you in a bright red work shirt and black trousers. You are beaming your bright smile at the camera. It looked as if you were beaming that smile directly at me.

I placed a finger on your hand in the photo and wished with all my powers of manifestation that you would somehow become real once again. Your smooth skin on mine, our fingers entwined. For hours I sat on the closet floor like this, crying, hoping, wishing, to no avail. You still remained out of reach. I wanted to die to be with you again.

I know I am not done with all I need to do here, and I want to make you proud, so I'll stay. But the hole you left behind keeps getting deeper. Whenever I think I have hit rock bottom, the floor comes out from under me once again. Will I ever stop falling?

The Tigger you clutched as a baby nearly thirty years ago sat next to the box containing your ashes. It was now faded and torn, stuffing spilling out of it much like the emotions spilled out of me. When we were apart during our engagement, I had its company each night and felt closer to you. After the accident, I slept with the sentimental stuffed animal once again. When I moved back to the States, I laid it to rest with you in my closet to keep you company. Last night, I clutched it tightly in my arms as I cried myself to sleep.

Love,
Aimee

Chapter 77

It's you there when I close my eyes
And you in the morning
I never thought you'd still be mine
Or I'd really need to have you around
—"The Real Thing," Gwen Stefani

London, 2007

As we near sleep, I rest my head on Ben's chest. His arm is wrapped tightly around me.

"I'm really proud of you, Aimee."

"Thanks, honey. I'm really proud of you too." I'm just drifting off and don't question him further.

He clarifies his statement anyway. "You really go after what you want, and it motivates me to want to do the same."

Having just earned my certification in life coaching, I am currently taking the necessary steps to be in business for myself. I pull free from sleep by stretching my arms and sitting up. "What is it you want to do, babe?"

"I don't know yet," Ben replies. I can hear him thinking. "While I'm happy where I am right now and gaining great experience, I would like to start my own business maybe five or ten years down the line."

"That's fantastic! I'm happy to support you in any and every way I can. Do you have any thoughts on what you would like to do?"

I can make out the crinkle in Ben's brow as he thinks about it. A few minutes pass. "Something to help people, but I'm not sure exactly what."

"Well, it will come to you when it's time. Whatever it is, I know you'll be great at it. You succeed at anything you put your mind to."

"Thanks, baby. I appreciate your support. I can't see myself staying at a company for twenty years or more. I'm sure I'll be doing something else." Ben looks slightly worried.

"I'm sure you will too," I agree, and give it some more serious thought. "You know, it's funny. I can usually see things when I imagine the future, but for some reason I can't see you not working for your current company. Weird, huh?"

"I was just thinking the same thing. I can't imagine it either. But, like I said, I can't imagine I would be staying there for decades."

We lie in silence, both trying to picture future Ben and what he will be doing.

After a few minutes, I'm still coming up blank. I look to Ben and see in his eyes that he is too.

"Well, maybe you continue to love it there so much you stay," I suggest, "or maybe we are just too tired to visualize."

"Maybe," Ben concurs and wraps his arm around me once again. I rest my head on his chest and give in to sleep.

Chapter 78

If someone said three years from now
You'd be long gone
I'd stand up and punch them out
'Cause they're all wrong
I know better
'Cause you said forever
And ever
Who knew?
—"Who Knew," Pink

Staunton, VA, July 17, 2011

Ben,

    I just woke up from a restful sleep in Staunton. The third anniversary of your passing landed on a weekend. I thought it best to take that as an opportunity to get away to someplace new. I could relax and leave any emotions that came out there, rather than letting them stagnate at home in Richmond.

    I knew the perfect place would find me, and it did. After doing an online search for B and Bs in Virginia, I came upon the perfect one that had all the amenities I required while being in an area that was easy to explore by foot. I booked a train ticket and was off to saunter around Staunton.

I'm staying in a room given the name "The Enchanted Cottage." The town is very quaint with lots of used bookstores, antique shops, and independent restaurants. I wandered around with a coffee in my hand and window-shopped, finding a used book I felt compelled to purchase.

For dinner, I headed into a cute little family-owned Mediterranean restaurant and asked to be seated near the window. Just as I sat down, a white-and-green motorbike whizzed past the window, the rider turning his head to look in my direction. The bike was very similar to yours. Were you whizzing past to check on me?

After dinner, I visited an antique shop on the main street. I passed a poster for the movie Moulin Rouge *and stared at it for a moment, seeing the synchronicities in our love stories. Then I was drawn to a painting of swirls of color, deep blues, purple, and yellow standing out most prominently. For some reason, I couldn't stop staring at this painting. I was mesmerized. Not wanting to carry a large painting home on the train with me, I finally walked away.*

Just as I was about to leave, the woman working at the store asked if I had found anything I liked. When I told her of the painting and my journey home on the train, she offered to pack it securely along with a handle to make it easy to carry. As an alternative, she offered to have it delivered.

It felt like it was meant to be, so I went to look at it again, now wondering about price. Oddly enough, I had taken on a new client the day before who had paid me the exact amount the painting was on offer for. Right next to the price was the title of the painting, "The Soul Between Lives." Wow, no wonder I couldn't stop staring at it! Did I need any more signs that this painting was coming home with me? No. I bought it on the spot, carrying it to the B and B easily, thanks to the owner's fantastic packaging skills.

When I arrived, I began to write and submitted my first short story (about us) to a writing competition. It was then I began to feel sad. I miss you.

To avoid shedding more tears, I opened up the book I had bought to read these words: "I had better spend more time singing and laughing and less time crying about the past."

Okay, Ben. I will.

All my love,
Aimee

Chapter 79

I did what I had to do and saw it through without exemption
I planned each charted course, each careful step along the byway
And more, much more than this, I did it my way
—"My Way," Frank Sinatra

London, December 2007

"Why don't we create something new this Christmas?"

"Sounds good! What did you have in mind?"

"How about having Christmas here? I'll cook!"

I love the idea. For one, Ben is an excellent cook, so I know the meal will be fantastic. My mouth is already watering even before knowing the menu. I really don't need any further reasons why this will be brilliant. I immediately agree.

Our usual Christmas routine alternates. We hop on a plane to the States every other year to spend the holidays with my family, and the rest of the years we spend driving to celebrate at the homes of Ben's family. One year we completely let go of all family obligations and had the best time spending Christmas alone together. Hosting and entertaining family in our own home is something I have not considered before. Now I wonder why it has never come to mind. This is going to be fun.

We go all out and buy a six-foot tree to replace the three-foot one we have used for Christmases past. For the menu, we watch Jamie Oliver's Christmas show, detailing his favorite holiday recipes. While I drool, Ben takes notes on how to perfectly cook a turkey and make magnificent side dishes, including my favorite, sage stuffing. To my great delight, chocolate truffles are for dessert.

Once the plans are set, Ben's mum and stepdad happily accept our invitation and agree to be our guests. Our first family Christmas at home. All going well, this may be the first of many.

The weeks leading up to the big day are filled with shopping trips for food and gifts for family and friends. By Christmas Eve, our fridge is stuffed as full as we plan to stuff the turkey.

The day goes off without a hitch. Our tiny kitchen explodes with the aromas of sage and spices and the cooking turkey while the living room is bursting with laughter and presents. Ben, Kevin, and I each wear a Santa hat. Alyson dons a headband with green-sequined reindeer antlers and red feathers. I entertain everyone with my Christmas decorations, including a walking reindeer wearing a Santa hat and carrying a bell that jingles, and a Frosty the Snowman at a piano singing Christmas carols.

Limited space on our kitchen counters leaves us little room for the tray of truffles, which Ben puts upstairs in our room until it's time to serve dessert. Being a chocolate connoisseur, I self-appoint myself as quality-control person and periodically pop upstairs to try a truffle. After eating about five, or maybe six, I feel confident that they are good enough to share with everyone.

By the end of the day, our bellies are full and ache from so much laughing. Alyson and Kevin leave with big smiles and some leftovers along with their gifts.

On a high from enjoying such a great day, as well as some bubbly, Ben and I agree it has been the perfect. The only thing missing is my dad. We decide to make a short video greeting to send to him so he can virtually enjoy the festivities.

Ben sets the camera to start recording. We both smile into the camera. I'm waiting for Ben to start, not aware he is waiting for me to do the same. Our smiles still plastered on our faces, Ben says under his breath, "Go . . . go," while keeping his smile intact. Instead, perhaps as a result of the bubbly, I burst into laughter. Ben shakes his head and sets up another take.

This time we are more prepared. As we hug each other, wearing our Santa hats in front of our six-foot, decorated Christmas tree, we smile into the camera and say, "Hello! Merry Christmas from London! Missing you! Looking forward to seeing you soon! Love you! Bye!"

It has been an incredible day, better than I ever could have dreamed. Little did I know it would be the last Christmas both Ben and Dad would be on this earth.

Chapter 80

I don't know where
Confused about how as well
Just know that these things
Will never change for us at all
—"Chasing Cars," Snow Patrol

Richmond, July 2011

"What on earth?" I said to myself in disbelief when I saw the picture that flashed on the screen.

I had just woken up from a very strange dream.

I was in a huge train station in England, only it didn't look like any station I had visited in the past. It was enclosed, spotlessly clean, and lined with red carpets. My brother and sister-in-law dropped me off there, but I wasn't sure where I was going. They said to get on the train to what sounded like "Banburro," but that was not a place I knew. They told me they were going for a hot-air balloon ride. I declined the offer to go with them. I was nervous as my phone was dying and I wouldn't be able to get in touch with them if I got lost. They said not to worry; they would call me if there was a problem . . . which I thought was odd as my phone would be dead. I wondered how they would get through, but they seemed confident . . .

Anyway, I went in and put my ticket through a handheld device that everyone was using to go through the enclosed gate. There were no signs for departures, but there was a well-dressed woman behind a desk, whom I assumed was there to give information. I asked, "Where do I get the train to Banburro?" She told me nicely that she didn't know and I needed to find it myself.

Slightly worried I would miss my train, I frantically rushed around while carrying two heavy suitcases. I asked more people, but no one knew. There were lots of train platforms, so my next step was to look at each platform and ask people. I left my suitcases with another well-dressed information lady and set off with a sense of dread building in my stomach.

As I entered one platform, a good friend of mine rushed in to save the day! She said to me, "Hey, matey, we wouldn't let you get lost!" She told me which platform I needed to be on. I was astounded and asked how she found me. She answered that her husband had put my name on a tracking device when I traveled. When I put my ticket in the handheld device, he saw it and she came to make sure I knew where to go.

Then I woke up, grateful for having such good friends, both in reality and in my dreams.

Too curious to stay lying down, I jumped out of bed and grabbed my laptop to find the location of this mysterious "Banburro." Unsure how to spell it, as everyone in my dream pronounced it slightly differently, my fingers decided on B-A-N-B-U-R-R-O, and I press Enter. Instantly before my eyes there appeared a picture of a castle that looked familiar. Incredibly familiar. Under the photo was the caption "Bamburgh Castle."

That was it. The place where Ben and I had our final picture taken together. Ben was lifting me up on the beach below the castle. We were smiling and carefree, my hair blowing in the wind, Ben's bright orange Oakley lenses reflecting the sunshine.

Over a year after the accident, my sister-in-law rediscovered these photographs on Ben's camera when I passed it on to her. Ben had only bought it a few months prior to his passing, and he was still working out all the features. Being a photographer, she had helped him choose the best camera to suit his needs and our budget. She printed the photos she found, and I gifted a set to Alyson for her birthday, framing an artistic shot of the castle with the sun shining down on it. An almost identical photo was now on my computer screen.

Bamburgh Castle. The name had escaped my memory, although I had been chasing it since sending the photo to Alyson. Just when I could feel it within my reach, it would slip from my fingers and disappear. I had all but given up the hunt when finally it came out of the shadows and into my dreams.

I sat staring in awe at the picture of the castle. Identical to Ben's photo. The picture that instantly came up, even when the word I typed in was horribly misspelled.

The pieces of my shattered world seemed to be coming back together again.

Chapter 81

Beautiful boy
How on earth did I do something worth deserving you?
My better half
How I cherish through and through every part of you
I do
—"Without You," Christina Aguilera

London to Iceland, January 2008

I wake up on my thirtieth birthday, excited to discover Ben's birthday surprise for me. It's even better than I could ever have imagined (and I have a wild imagination). He reveals he has booked us a trip to Iceland! And we are leaving in a few hours! It's a mad rush to pack. Soon we are off on a new adventure.

We arrive to experience the magic of Iceland. There is something significantly different about this trip in relation to those we have taken in the past. Normally we are rushed and trying hard to please one another, always looking for more to see, always trying to impress. For some reason, this time we are both completely relaxed. As we board a bus to Reykjavik, we hold one another's hands and absorb our surroundings in stunned silence. We gaze at one another and smile, completely at peace.

This calm lasts throughout the four days we are there. We embrace the cold and culture of Iceland, exploring the terrain of volcanoes and waterfalls, dining on fine food, and bathing in geothermal pools, the warmth heating our bodies while snowflakes kiss our cheeks.

One afternoon we witness a heavy storm in the distance. We watch from the comfort of our hotel room as the dark cloud spewing heavy rain and snow makes its way across the city. We hold on to each other tightly, oblivious that the biggest storm of my life is just around the corner.

Chapter 82

And I wonder how I never got the burn
And if I'm ever gonna learn
How lonely people make a life
One strain at a time and still shine
—"The Burn," Matchbox Twenty

Richmond, August 2011

I had just arrived home from my "office' at Starbucks. I set down my red laptop carrying case/backpack on the couch. As I turned around, the room started to rumble.

I looked up, thinking it was my upstairs neighbor's washing machine on a vicious spin cycle. But it felt too strong, so I stepped to the doorway to look out. I saw other houses shaking too. This was surreal. I'd never known there to be earthquakes in Richmond, Virginia. What was going on?

As I stood in the doorway a few seconds later, it was all over. Had I just dreamed that? Was I going crazy?

I took out my laptop and logged on. Thank God for Facebook and Twitter. Richmond had just had an earthquake, they confirmed. Well, at least I was not going crazy.

That was certainly unexpected. It wasn't the first time my world had been shaken.

Chapter 83

And Edison would spin in his grave
To ever see the light that you gave
Don't wanna take it nice and slow here
Don't wanna waste a minute more dear
—"Warmer Climate," Snow Patrol

February 2008

"No, you mean benign, Dad. Malignant is the bad one."

"No, no. Malignant is the one I meant," Dad confirms nonchalantly on the phone.

My heart falls to my knees, and the world I know starts crashing down around me.

April 2008

My dad's health has taken a turn for the worse. Ben and I board a plane at London Heathrow and arrive at Detroit Metro Airport. After picking up our luggage and passing through customs and immigration, we enter the arrivals area. My eyes search the crowd, looking for a familiar face. As I watch families and friends embrace their reunion, the realization hits me. No one is there to greet us.

I struggle to hold back tears. This is the first time I have arrived in my hometown without seeing my dad's smiling face and feeling his warm embrace. I realize this will never happen again. Ever. Ben senses my despair and puts on a brave smile. He wraps a comforting arm around me as we wait for my brother to pick us up.

We arrive at the house. Dad is too weak to come to the door and greet us. He is waiting in the back room, and I am shocked to the core when I see him. Always a robust man, he sits rail-thin and frail in a chair that looks to be devouring him. He stands briefly but is too weak to do so for long. I gather all my strength and willpower to keep the tears reined in.

Later that evening, I sob uncontrollably in Ben's arms. This has been going on for months. I hold in the river of tears through the day, the dam breaks in the darkness, and I cry through the night.

A few days later, we all visit the funeral home so Dad can make his own arrangements.

As we leave, Dad turns around and directs a question to the funeral director. "My daughter and son-in-law live in England. When the day does come, it will take them a day or two to get back for the funeral. Can you put me on ice until they arrive?"

Ben and I, along with the rest of the family, stand with mouths gaping, in shock at the flippant reference.

The funeral director immediately puts my father and the rest of us at ease. "Don't worry, Mr. DuFresne. Your daughter and son-in-law will be here," she says. Ben and I nod our heads.

As we step outside, Dad nudges Ben's shoulder from behind and tells him, "I don't want you to miss the party." He smiles.

"Wouldn't miss it for the world, Jerry," Ben assures him.

In the days that follow, Dad's health deteriorates drastically. He is forced to swap the comfy bed in his home for a standard, sterile hospital bed. It is located in a cold room at the end of a long hall illuminated by blinding fluorescent light.

Ben and I, along with my two older brothers, stand uncomfortably in the hallway. Dad has finally drifted to sleep. We stand outside the room so as not to disturb him, but we don't drift far in case he wakes and needs our assistance. No words are spoken. We shift from one foot to the other, each of us lost in our own thoughts. The bright lights are shining a spotlight on my biggest fear: losing someone I love so much.

"Ben?" a weak voice questions from the darkened room. Then a bit louder, "Ben!" We all look at each other in surprise. Ben rushes in to aid my father.

Dad's preference for Ben's assistance continues as he is moved from hospital to hospice. Ben is happy to oblige. He is patient, kind, and encouraging—a lot like my dad would be if the situation had been reversed. Ben jokes and makes him laugh. It makes me love the both of them even more than I already do.

Ben helps Dad during the day and holds me at night while I sob my way to sleep. He does it all without complaint, without an unkind word for anyone. He is an angel.

I share with Ben my fear that Dad will no longer recognize or remember me. Seeing him so frail is hard enough. I'm not sure I can take it if he doesn't know who I am. Every day when we arrive at the hospice, I am grateful that his memory is intact.

One day, as I sit on one side of Dad's bed and Ben on the other, Dad's bright blue eyes look at mine questioningly. He leans in close and asks, "Who is that?" His eyes shift to the chair in which Ben sits.

My breath is taken from me. My worst fear becomes reality.

I gather up enough strength to say in a small voice, "Dad, that's Ben. That's my husband."

Dad turns his head around to see. "Yeah, I know that's Ben!" Dad is exasperated and shakes his head. "Who is the other guy?"

he whispers, making another gesture to the empty space behind Ben.

"There is just Ben there," I say. "Who do you see there? What does he look like?" I'm glad he still recognizes Ben but curious who else he sees where the rest of us only see open space.

"Nothing. Never mind." Dad closes his eyes to end any further inquiry.

Almost four weeks after our arrival in Detroit, Dad passes over late in the night. That night I refuse to leave, and the whole family decides to stay at the hospice. Just as I start to drift into sleep, Dad takes his last breath. A hand on my arm gently shakes me awake, and I open my eyes for the first time to a world without my father.

Near the end, talking and breathing were difficult. His body deteriorated. He was unrecognizable as the man he once was before the illness. But during all that time, I could still see the dad I knew when I looked into his eyes or was just in his presence. I knew he was there, stuck in a body that was no longer working.

When I open my eyes this time, although I see Dad's body lying on the bed, I can feel Dad is gone. It feels as if he has just gotten up and left the room. He no longer needs this shell. He is free.

Less than twenty-four hours and an infinite number of tears later, I sit quietly on the couch, giving myself a pep talk in my head so I can help my brother, sister-in-law, and Ben make the dreaded phone calls telling people the news.

But I can't do it.

Ben ends up making the most calls. When the task is complete, we all sit at the table. They share their experiences, and I am glad I did not participate in the calls. I can barely deal with my own pain, much less someone else's. Ben lightens the mood by telling us that many people couldn't understand his British accent, which made the task rather tricky.

A few days later is the funeral. The party Dad did not want Ben to miss. It is the very first funeral I have ever attended. Too overcome by sorrow, I refrain from getting up to speak. Ben takes the lead. He stands in front of the people to pay his last respects and share the story of how he met my father. True to form, he gives a great talk. Everyone laughs as Ben recounts how he was sweating profusely due to nerves when his five feet six self looked up to Dad's six feet five stature. How he was reprimanded when he was caught kissing me at the theater where we were seeing Fosse. How he refused to even hold my hand for the rest of the night, only to find out later that my father was only joking.

When Ben is not on stage speaking, he is holding on to my hand tightly as the tears flow down my face. I am so grateful for Ben. When I tell him this and thank him, he answers simply, with tears in his own eyes, "He was my dad too."

Never in my deepest sorrow could I imagine that in a few short months I will be at another funeral, my hands and heart empty. Both my best friends go to the afterlife party, while I am stuck back on earth, anxiously awaiting my own invitation.

Chapter 84

If I lay here
If I just lay here
Would you lie with me
And just forget the world?
—"Chasing Cars," Snow Patrol

Richmond, July 2011

I had it in my mind, though subconsciously as the years passed, that if I was good enough, nice enough, kind enough, smart enough, brave enough, and tried hard enough to make a difference, then that would be it. I would earn my ticket to be with Ben and Dad again. After every success in my new life, no matter how small or seemingly insignificant, I would write in my journal to Ben the same words: *"Are you ready for me yet?"*

Given I was still here, I guessed the answer was no. "Are you even listening to me down here?" I asked the open air one day before going out on a dinner date. I thought maybe I needed to prove I could have fun here before being admitted to the big party.

We headed to a Mexican restaurant with an outdoor patio on a main street. It was a gorgeous day, and dining outside was the perfect way to enjoy it. My date was dubious we would get a table outside, but I confidently told him there would be one table for two available for us when we arrived.

The patio was crowded with diners soaking up the sunshine, but I was right and there was one empty table among the crowd. We sat down and ordered drinks. While we waited quietly, I overheard the couple beside us talking. My ears perked up at the mention of Heathrow. I thought it was interesting there was mention of a place near where I had lived for so long.

We kept up our own conversation, so I wasn't really listening to theirs. But I would catch a few things about what she was saying about her trip to London, and how Heathrow was so busy and it took forever for the plane to taxi in from the runway. It brought back memories, and I smiled to myself.

Realizing I was rather ignoring my date, I made a greater effort. We chatted over our dinner. Then I heard the man at the other table say something much closer to home than Heathrow: "Ben Morgan. Well, that's a common name. Type 'Ben Morgan' in Google and you'll get many results. A lot of people are called Ben Morgan." The man said Ben's name *three times*! Granted, it was without the "s" of "Morgans." but really, what were the chances? I froze for a minute when I heard him say this. I couldn't believe it. Their conversation changed after that, and I kept my thoughts to myself.

That was until I got home. I called my mom for her opinion. She was as shocked as I was. She definitely thought it was a sign, but was unsure as to the message. I e-mailed Alyson for her opinion.

Then I took out my notebook, my direct line to Ben, and wrote, *What are you trying to tell me, Ben? Other than reminding me Mexican food was your favorite.*

I felt I was missing the key to some important message that would change everything.

Chapter 85

And it's true that you've reached a better place
Still I'd give the world to see your face
—"Bye Bye," Mariah Carey

Detroit-London, April 2008

A few days following the funeral, Ben and I collapse into our economy seats for our eight-hour journey back to London. It still doesn't seem real that I will never see my father again. He had promised he would visit and see our new home. In all my life, he had never broken a promise. I wonder how he plans on keeping this one now. There must be a sign he will send from the other side to let me know he is there. How will I know it is from him?

I keep these thoughts to myself as Ben takes off his shoes, puts on the complimentary eye mask, and pushes back his seat shortly after takeoff to get some long-overdue rest. It amazes me how he can always fall asleep so easily on planes. Flipping through the in-flight magazine, I send a mental message to my father. I ask him to be sure his signal is clear so that I will know it is him when he is there. Then I settle on a movie to help pass the time as Ben sleeps soundly beside me.

When we arrive at Heathrow, air traffic is heavy. The plane has to circle a few times before landing. This is expected, as it happens nearly every time we travel into Heathrow, but it is still frustrating to me to be so close, only to go for another loop around the sky.

When we finally land, we go through immigration together and wait to pick up our luggage. Then we pass through customs and finally out to the fresh air. As soon as we step outside, I am looking around for Dad's sign. Surely he will send something immediately to let me know he has kept his promise.

I looked at the cars whizzing by and the crowds of people around me. Nothing. No sign in sight.

On the shuttle bus en route to our car in the long-term parking lot, I call my boss to tell him I am back. He is surprised to learn I am still planning on attending the raw food school that weekend. Surely I need to take some time to grieve, he says.

I feel like I've been grieving for years. If Dad's death has taught me anything, it is to live in the moment. If not now, when? I will learn a lot at the school. If I can help just one person become healthier and avoid cancer with this knowledge, it will be worth it. I can't think of a better way to honor my dad's memory and move on with life, as he taught me to do.

Once home, we lug our heavy bags upstairs. I look around for the sign from Dad, not knowing exactly what I am looking for but confident that once I see it, I'll know. Too exhausted to unpack and not seeing any sign, I lie down on our bed and immediately fall asleep. After tossing and turning on a pull-out couch for a month, I am grateful to be back in my own bed. It's almost like this whole mess never happened. Maybe when I wake up, Dad will be alive and healthy once again.

What feels like minutes but in actuality is hours later, Ben's voice repeats softly in my ear, "Aimee. Aimee. It's time to wake up." He gently rocks my shoulders. I open my eyes a slit, enough to see his beautiful face. "We have to get up, Aimee. We have to go soon."

We have tickets to a Matchbox 20 concert. We have both wanted to see the band for years, but either tickets had been sold out or we were out of town. At the beginning of this year, when tickets went on sale, we were delighted to finally have the opportunity to go. That was before Dad's health took a turn for the worse. While we were in Michigan, we had both long forgotten about it. But, as it is, the concert is on the day we arrive home. We think we should take a leaf out of the book of Dad and live life to the fullest by going.

My eyelids feel like lead, but Ben the warrior helps me fight them open. While I was sleeping, Ben unpacked all our belongings, went food shopping, and caught up on the mail. My gratitude comes with the sneaking feeling that even if I never sleep again, I probably still won't get as much done as Ben does. I wonder where he gets his superpowers and if one day they will magically rub off on me too.

Dragging myself to the shower and rustling up some clean clothes, I manage to get ready for the concert. It might not be as involved as unpacking, shopping, or cleaning, but for me, it's quite a feat. I'm proud when we get in the car with time to spare.

The sun is shining after a little rain. I keep looking around for Dad's sign. C'mon, Dad! You *said* you would visit me here. You promised!

Keeping this dialogue internal and my search for a sign a secret, I sigh in the seat next to Ben. I continue my internal rant. He is not sending a sign. He is not here. I'm stupid to believe he would be. What would the sign he sends look like anyway?

Just as these thoughts fill my head, Ben exclaims, "Look at the rainbow, Aimee!" and points out the window at the most glorious rainbow I have ever seen.

"That's Dad!" I exclaim, clapping my hands. I know with every cell in my being that the rainbow is indeed the sign Dad is sending to let me know he is still with me.

A mask of confusion covers Ben's face. He has no idea what I'm talking about. I explain, and he nods his head slowly, trying to decide if I have gone off the deep end since losing my dad.

In the following weeks, I can feel Dad's presence everywhere. While I am walking to work or brushing my teeth, I can sense him. Sometimes the scent of him wafts around me.

Ben humors me during this time, though I can tell he thinks perhaps I am on the verge of a breakdown. My tears continue to flow, and I try to hide them from Ben as much as possible. Panic attacks strike me at the oddest times, like when we are dropping off our recycling at the local center. I can't control the sudden stream of tears running down my face; fear strikes my heart and it hurts to breathe.

Ben's kind eyes meet mine each time. He holds my hand and repeats, "Just breathe. I'm right here. You're okay. Just breathe."

His calm manner helps me through. While I am getting used to a world without my dad, my fear of losing Ben increases every day. During my plethora of panic attacks, I repeat, "Don't leave me. Promise me you'll never leave me. You are the only one here who really knows me."

My mantra is always the same and so is Ben's. "I'm right here. I'm not going anywhere. I'm always right here."

Chapter 86

'Cause sometimes we don't really notice
Just how good it can get
So maybe we should start all over
Start all over again
—"Someday," Rob Thomas

Richmond, August 2011

There I was in a house that had had three floods, two gas leaks, and, I had just found out, a mold issue.

It was time to find a new home.

I sat down with a paper and pen and asked myself what I wanted in my new home. While I was at it, I thought I should enjoy it, and what was the harm of writing down all the amenities I desired? What did I want?

The list began with more space, mold-free, flood-free, less expensive rent, heat included, a parking space, on-site laundry, and outdoor space, and it went on from there.

Now that I knew what I wanted, I started looking at apartments. The first few apartments I viewed had exactly none of the things I was looking for. The search continued and my confidence began to wane. Maybe a mold-infested, flooded apartment wasn't so bad after all?

On a Sunday, I got an e-mail back from one building manager who told me I could see the place that day. He included a list of rules for renting. Although I abided by those rules anyway, I was a little taken aback that he had been so forthright before I had even seen the place. Expecting it to be similar to the rest of the apartments I have viewed, I wasn't excited, but I talked myself, as well as a friend, into going to see it.

When we walked in the door, I was amazed. It had everything on my list except for on-site laundry, and the closest laundry was only a block away. When the building manager told me he intended to rent the place that day, whether to me or someone else, I knew he was serious. This place was going to go fast, given its vast space, inexpensive rent, and great location. I signed the lease immediately. After all, it was only missing one thing on my long list of demands.

I moved in, and a few months later a washing machine and dryer were installed in the basement.

Wow. If I could manifest this, what else could I do? What did I want to do?

Suddenly, the world seemed much more open to possibility.

Chapter 87

All this feels strange and untrue
And I won't waste a minute without you
My bones ache, my skin feels cold
And I'm getting so tired and so old
—"Open Your Eyes," Snow Patrol

London, May 2008

"What shall we do to celebrate next year's wedding anniversary?" Ben queries.

Our five-year wedding anniversary was spent in the hospice caring for Dad, hoping, praying, and silently pleading he would not take his final breath on the very day we had got married. Thankfully, our prayers were answered. Dad left his body on a day midway between our wedding anniversary and that of my brother and his wife.

"I don't know about next year, but we are still on for our ten-year anniversary, when we will renew our vows, yes?"

Not long after we got married, we began planning for our ten-year anniversary, when we intend to renew our vows. We want it to be something special, just for us, in a magical place. We have toyed with many ideas, including something tacky in Vegas, complete with plastic flowers and a drive-through chapel, or inside with an Elvis impersonator saying, "You can kiss the bride, uh-huh, uh-huh." We have laughed at the idea for a long time but decide on something a bit classier: a secluded beach in Hawaii. It will be perfect.

"Of *course* we are on for our ten-year anniversary in Hawaii!" Ben confirms. "Only five more years to go. It will be here before we know it!"

As I walk to work, I paint the picture of the day in my mind. I can clearly see the beach and the sun shining overhead. Then a vision comes to my mind. Dressed in a strapless white-and-gold frock, a huge smile on my face, I can see what appears to be a self-taken photo of two of us. My face looks slightly more mature, my blonde hair now dark brown. I look immensely happy. But when I search for Ben's face beside me, it is blank. I cannot see a face, only light. Did the flash cut him out? Why can't I see him?

Examining this vision more closely in my mind's eye, I see dark hair, although I still can't make out a face. Ben's hair is light brown, nothing like what I see. My ability to visualize is exceptional, and it disturbs me I cannot see Ben's smiling face next to my own.

I take a deep breath as I enter the clinic and close my eyes for a moment, hoping the visualization will be clearer then. It is not.

As I walk up the two flights of stairs to the door of the clinic, I refuse to believe Ben is not in the picture. Mentally, I take an image of Ben and cut out the head, pasting it next to mine in my vision of our Hawaiian wedding. It looks wrong. Ben's face has not aged at all. It looks like an old photo cut and pasted.

But I reach the top of the stairs, and this cut-and-paste vision will have to do, as I now need to concentrate on work. I'm left to wonder about the identity of the man with the dark hair.

To ease my anxiety, I keep telling myself it is only a silly vision. Of course Ben will be there with me on our tenth anniversary in Hawaii. After all, my hair is blonde, not dark as I saw in the picture. Clearly, my visualizing mastery has dimmed since my father's death.

I take a deep breath and continue to see the pasted image of Ben's young face next to my own. I promise myself to make the effort to get my excellent visualization skills back so I can see us clearly again.

A shiver runs through me as I shake off the vision, even though the room is warm.

Chapter 88

Oh this is my song
I'm just like you
I gotta fight to stay strong
Just 'cause it clears
It don't mean that it's over
I'm a shine
While my lights on
—"Shine," Estelle

Richmond, December 2011

The storms and hurricane season had passed and winter was setting in. Christmas was coming. For years as a child, I used to write a letter to Santa asking for everything I wanted. On Christmas Day, most of those items would be wrapped and waiting for me under the tree.

What if life were like that? When had it stopped being magical? I'd got this apartment, after all, with all the amenities I desired. What if I put that creative energy into the rest of my life?

I looked at my life, all areas, and asked myself, what did I love to do? What was I doing now that I didn't love? If I could do, be, or have anything within my desire, what would it be?

I found there were parts of my life I was happy with, parts that could be dramatically better, and parts that didn't really fit me at all, yet I continued to do them. Why? What if I stopped doing what I didn't love and focused all my attention on things that I did? What if I loved all my life? Could it be possible? What did I have to lose by trying?

My mind wandered back to my first job, working for my dad. I loved being with my dad but hated working retail. When I brought this to his attention, he gave me an option to quit along with a piece of advice. "Look, whatever you decide to do, remember that you won't always want to go to work. Sometimes there are things in life that you don't want to do, but you have to do, so you do them anyway." Had I taken Dad's advice too literally?

Memories of his final days came to me then. Dad and I are sitting at the kitchen table. He tells me he is proud of me. He says he is happy I am enjoying life with Ben. Then he says something that will stay with me forever. "I have no regrets. I'm happy with all my decisions. I love my life. My career as a pharmacist was the best job for me. I wouldn't change a thing."

His words then motivated me to change my career to something more fulfilling. But was it fulfilling me now? My life was good, but could it be better? Could it be great? I knew there were areas where I was "settling," and areas I kept putting off for "later." But I knew full well that now is all we ever have.

If today were my last day, the one I had begged Ben for in my journal to him for so long, would I have regrets?

The answer was yes, I would. And the time was now to start doing something to change that.

Chapter 89

Down from edge, I can see where we end
I'd give up all my days to go back
There was all this wonder, and all this magic
Is all this wonder, over and done?
—"I Can't Let You Go," Matchbox Twenty

July 16, 2008

Grabbing Ben's orthotics, I rush downstairs on my way to work. Hearing me clatter down the stairs, Ben puts down his weights momentarily and meets me at the foot.

"Oh yay! You remembered to take my orthotics in! Thanks, baby!"

"Of course! My pleasure."

We kiss.

"I love you!"

"I love you too! Oh! Remember, I am out tonight with work. Quiz night. I'll be home by eleven or eleven thirty at the latest. Don't wait up!" Ben picks up his weights to resume his workout.

"Kick some ass, honey," I say with a wink.

"Oh yes," says Ben. "I intend to win." He beams a smile back at me between the deep breaths as he completes his bicep curls.

Closing the door behind me, I step into the clear day outside and begin my thirty-minute walk to work, thinking to myself, "I love my life."

It is my last full-time day working at the clinic. To give me time to focus on growing my life-coaching practice, I have cut down my hours there. Excitement is in the air. I finally feel like I'm getting closer to doing the work that I love and am meant to be doing.

Time seems to go in slow motion, which is quite a contrast to what we have been experiencing lately. Ben even mentioned a few days earlier that time seems to be moving too fast. We are both so busy with work, the fundraising group I have started, and other, miscellaneous activities that eat up a lot of our time. Now that I will be working less at the clinic, I hope it would result in a few extra hours of quality time together.

Afternoon finally arrives, and I am out the door on my way home. As part of my offering to new coaching clients, I want to include healthy food prep. So I get to work on some healthy and delicious food. I am great at making healthy food. As far as delicious goes . . . well, I'm working on that. Ben is my official taste tester and not always an easy critic to please, especially as he has natural talent in the cooking department.

I find a recipe for walnut burgers and go straight into the kitchen, getting out ingredients and hoping the results meet with his approval. Thinking how fantastic it will be to impress him, I carefully execute the recipe exactly as written, not wanting to mess it up. Once the walnut "meat" is prepped into patties, I place them on a tray and pop them in the oven, hoping for the best.

Knowing Ben loves citrus juices, I peel some satsumas to juice for him the following morning. Finished in the kitchen, I head upstairs to check my e-mail. There is one from a friend who has invited me to check out a raw vegan festival near Oxford. It sounds like fun to me. Forwarding the details to Ben, I write,

"This is probably not your thing, but I thought I would send it on to see if you might be interested. ;-) Love, Aimee."

There is no response. Ben has mentioned how busy he is at work, so I'm not surprised. I sent the e-mail as a heads up so we can discuss it tomorrow.

Even though I don't expect to hear from him, I check my e-mail a few more times, hoping maybe he will send a response. I miss him. Still no reply, so I continue with my coaching work. When the mail comes, I'm hoping it brings my new business cards with the logo Ben suggested I have designed. I can't wait to see them.

The post comes, but the business cards do not. It's dinnertime. I snag one of the freshly made walnut burgers and make a large green salad to go with it. I add some barbecue sauce Ben made a few days earlier. Surprisingly, whether it's due to the burger or the sauce, the meal is delicious. I think Ben might actually enjoy this! I'm excited for him to try it and curious about his reaction. A little disappointed he has a social function with work, although I'm sure he is having fun.

I watch some television before heading to bed. Ben said he would be home by eleven thirty at the latest, but my eyes are having trouble staying open past ten thirty. I've been up since five this morning. Upstairs, I wash my face and brush my teeth. Telling myself perhaps I'll read until he gets home, I get into bed. But before I can even reach over to turn on the reading lamp, my head finds the pillow and my mind drifts off to dreamland.

Oddly enough, it is the first time I have fallen asleep so easily without Ben beside me. Normally I would toss and turn, keeping an ear out for his motorbike in the driveway.

But that night I fall asleep immediately and sleep soundly until an insistent knock breaks my slumber and changes my life.

Epilogue

And I'll forget the world that I knew
But I swear I won't forget you
Oh if my voice could reach back through the past
I'd whisper in your ear:
"Oh darling I wish you were here"
—"Vanilla Twilight," Owl City

I am in a movie theater. The lights are low and all my
attention is focused on the screen. Suddenly, it is the end of the
movie. The lights come up. Nothing has changed but everything
is different.

Ben was the main character in my life. When he died, I realized I was surrounded by people I knew were there in the theater with me. But I had never really seen them before. I was too focused on what was happening on the big screen.

We left the theater. I kept in touch with some of the people who had been watching the movie with me. Others went their separate ways. All the while, I kept hoping to see the movie again. The memory of it played over and over in the confines of my mind. Surely there would be a sequel. Everyone else went to other movies and kept going with their lives. I pretended to watch, but nothing else held my attention in quite the same way. I stumbled from one movie screen to the next, unsure what I wanted to see and who I wanted to see. Nothing compared to that movie I loved so much.

It was years later before I finally woke up to life.

I made a decision. I was no longer watching life. I was living it.

Listening to my favorite spiritual radio station one day while preparing food, I discovered how to make a "miracle box." You wrote down what you wanted in life on pieces of paper, adding them to the box. Having given this very subject a lot of thought recently, I began to write. Note after note went into the box: things I wanted in my career, ways I wanted to help others, principles by which I wanted to live my life, and more ideas for my finances, my home, and even my love life.

I wrote on one piece of paper, "I am in a deeply loving relationship with a wonderful man who loves me infinitely, and I love him in return."

Once written, I looked at the tiny piece of paper and snorted out laughter. This was so far-fetched. But I took a moment and continued to look at it. I felt in my body and mind how wonderful it would be if this were a fact.

In the days following this ritual, things started working on my behalf. Setting financial fears aside, I agreed to travel to New York City for Christmas with a friend. We found a cheap deal on travel, and another friend who lived in the city offered us her apartment to stay in without charge.

The years ahead were going to be magical. This I knew because I was going to make them so.

Even when the sun did not shine overhead, I realized no one could take away my internal sunshine. It was up to me to make it shine brightly through the foggy uncertainty of life. With the beams of my light, who knew what I would discover that had always been there, cloaked in the darkness?

I was ready to find out.

Time stretched ahead of me like an infinitely long red carpet. No longer would I race forward, eyes always focused ahead, hoping to finally see the finish line. No. Instead I would swap my sweaty running gear for my best dress and walk the carpet in sparkly shoes, smiling, laughing, and enjoying myself. I chose now to really see all that surrounded me, rather than squinting ahead, trying to decipher where it all would end.

I was exactly where I was meant to be. Right here. Right now. Now I was choosing to savor every delicious moment.

Finally, it dawned on me. Even when you can't see the sun shining, it does not cease to exist. It is still there. Always. Just like my Ben.

Afterword

W riting this book was quite an emotional journey. During the process, I cried an ocean of tears and drank a river of wine. The story remained in my head and on my to-do list, untouched or briefly picked up, to be put down again in an effort to focus on rebuilding my new life.

After falling in love again and getting remarried (yes, I found that dark-haired man from my vision, thanks to that miracle box), I felt the story was infecting me. It was time to share it with the world. With the support of my second husband (my "Moon"), I finally made the time and committed myself to finishing the book and sharing it with the world.

The intention behind structuring the story in jumps is that it mirrors how I felt emotionally during that time. I was drowning in memories of my love story with Ben. I would hit the surface of reality, only to be pulled back under, deeper, and spit out again, all the while hoping one day to reach the shore of my new life.

My intent in sharing this is the hope that you realize how resilient you are. Dig deep enough and believe. I believe in you. All of us have this light inside us, this internal sunshine. Sometimes life hits the dimmer switch, and we think the light has gone out. But it is on. We have the ability to make it shine brightly and last forever. Keep Going.

About the Author

Kicking off her thirtieth birthday with a surprise celebration in Iceland, Aimee DuFresne was oblivious to the fact that the year would soon be filled with tragedy and unimaginable heartbreak.

In the next 12 months Aimee lost the two most significant men in her life: her ailing father and her young husband. In her deepest state of grief, Aimee realized she had a choice: she could simply give up or she could fight to keep going. She began letting go of fears to live her life to the fullest and realized her dream of being an author, a speaker, a radio show host and healthy living chef. After transforming her own life, she now empowers other women around the world to do the same. Need guidance to keep going? Join Aimee and the Keep Going Movement at www.aimeedufresne.com.